MEET EDITH STEIN

Meet Edith Stein

*From Cloister to Concentration Camp,
a Carmelite Nun Confronts the Nazis*

CYNTHIA CAVNAR

SERVANT
BOOKS

PUBLISHED BY ST. ANTHONY MESSENGER PRESS
CINCINNATI, OHIO

Published by St. Anthony Messenger Press
28 W. Liberty St.
Cincinnati, OH 45202
www.servantbooks.com

Cover design: Paul Higdon, Minneapolis, Minn.
Cover photo: Catholic News Service

04 05 10 9 8 7 6 5 4 3 2

Printed in the United States of America
ISBN 1-56955-284-3

Library of Congress Cataloging-in-Publication Data

Cavnar, Cindy.
    Meet Edith Stein : from cloister to concentration camp, a Carmelite
    nun confronts the Nazis / Cynthia Cavnar.
        p. cm.
    Includes bibliographical references.
    ISBN 1-56955-284-3 (alk. paper)
        1. Stein, Edith, Saint, 1891-1942. 2. Carmelite Nuns--Germany--Biography.
    3. Philosophers--Germany--Biography. I.
    Title.
    BX4705.S814 C38 2002
    282'.092--dc21

                                                            2002006233

Contents

Introduction

"Into the East"

Captain S. Payne Best, a British intelligence specialist, sat out most of World War II in Nazi prisons. Having abducted him from his hotel in Venlo, the Netherlands, in 1939, the Germans deprived the allies of his expertise. But they unwittingly provided posterity with something else: insight into the Nazi mind. Payne kept a detailed diary.

His book, *The Venlo Incident,* recounts one of his more surrealistic moments at Buchenwald concentration camp in Germany. The Captain was assigned to a bunker for privileged prisoners. There he met Dr. Sigmund Rascher. "A queer fellow," Best later recalled, "possibly the queerest character which has ever come my way." [1]

Rascher was a medical doctor and a member of the personal staff for Heinrich Himmler, chief of Hitler's feared "security units" (known as the "SS"). This doctor was responsible for the gruesome medical experiments carried out on prisoners at Dachau death camp. He also planned and supervised the construction of the gas chambers there.

Although Rascher had fallen out of favor, he had a soft spot for the notorious Himmler. Himmler was "kind-hearted," Rascher insisted, and "most anxious that prisoners should be exterminated in a manner which caused them least anxiety and suffering." To that end, "the greatest trouble had been taken to design a gas chamber so camouflaged that its purpose would not be apparent and to regulate the flow of lethal gas so that the patients might fall asleep without recognizing that they would never wake."[2]

Unfortunately, Rascher admitted, the Nazis "had never quite succeeded in solving the problem caused by the varying resistance of different people to the effects of poison gas, and always there had been a few who lived longer than the others and recognized where they were and what was happening."

Those few, according to Rudolf Hoess, commander of Auschwitz concentration camp, actually numbered about two thirds of the people packed into a gas chamber. Hoess occasionally watched the process through a peephole. The approximately one third who were standing next to the airshaft where the poison was introduced "were killed immediately. The remainder staggered about and began to scream and struggle for air. The screams, however, soon changed to gasping." After about twenty minutes, all were dead.

Zyklon B, a form of hydrogen cyanide, was Hitler's gas of choice for "the Final Solution": the destruction of European Jewry. By mid-1941, between one and two million Jews had been killed by various means—starved, shot, gassed in specially rigged vans—but their systematic elimination only began in earnest in 1942. With the construction of new concentration camps and the expansion of existing ones, the stage was set. Thousands of Jews began arriving by the trainload at places such as Treblinka, Sobibor, and Belzec. Guards immediately herded most into the death chambers, although they spared a few for labor.

On August 9, 1942, a train from the Netherlands pulled up to Auschwitz and disgorged onto the platform over nine hundred exhausted, anxious Jews. Edith Stein and her sister, Rosa, both converts from Judaism to Catholicism, were among the weary travelers. Edith was a philosopher and a Carmelite nun known in the religious life as Sr. Teresa Benedicta of the Cross. Rosa was a Third Order Carmelite and worked at the Carmelite convent in Echt, Holland, where both women lived. They had fled there from their native Germany in the face of growing Nazi pressure.

In fact, hundreds of Catholics of Jewish descent were in this particular transport. They had been targeted for "deportation to the East" (a Nazi cover-up for extermination) in retaliation for the way the courageous Dutch Catholic Church had stood up to Nazi policies. Specifically, the Catholic bishops had issued a pastoral letter condemning the persecution and deportation of Jews. In direct defiance of Nazi orders, priests read the letter from every pulpit on Sunday, July 26, 1942.

The Nazis responded swiftly: "We, for our part, are compelled to regard Catholic Jews as our worst enemies and consequently see to their deportation to the East with all possible speed."[3]

It is ironic that Stein, an intellectual who used words very precisely, should disappear under a flurry of euphemisms: part of the "Final Solution" sent into "the East" for "special treatment," another Nazi code for murder. But there was nothing euphemistic about the gas that poured into the airtight room where she stood, naked, with her fellow victims. (Gas chambers were disguised as showers able to accommodate dozens of people at a time.) We know nothing about her final moments, but we do know that she was physically strong and mentally tough. She probably realized what was coming.

At the Nuremberg Trials held after the war, a former prisoner from Auschwitz recalled the words of another prisoner with a particularly grisly job—hauling the still-warm bodies out of the gas chamber. "They must have suffered before they died," he said of the scene that invariably greeted him, "because they clung together in bunches like grapes so that it was difficult to separate them."

A Jew, a Catholic, a Saint

When they pulled Edith Stein out of that room, she was one of millions of Jews to meet a similar fate. But she was also a Catholic, targeted as such in retaliation for the steely resolve of the Dutch Catholic Bishops. In the eyes of the Church, she was a martyr because she died in an action motivated by hatred for the faith. She herself had anticipated this possibility. In 1939, Edith had prophetically offered her life as a sacrificial prayer of reparation for the sins of the Nazi era.

As a child, Edith once wrote, she was convinced she was "destined for something great." Her fate confirmed her earlier intuition, although not in a way she could have imagined in the innocent years before Nazism. Nor was it a way that has turned out to be particularly comfortable for either Catholics or Jews.

When Edith was canonized, many Jews opposed her canonization. They were troubled that the Church would single out for sainthood a woman they consider an apostate. Couldn't the Church honor other Christian victims of the Germans instead? Actually, some Jews wondered why the Church would canonize Christian victims of the Nazis at all. They felt that such gestures obscured the specific intent of the Holocaust, total destruction of the Jews.

The Church, on the other hand, took into account not only Edith's martyrdom but also her own understanding of her Jewish-Catholic identity. After her conversion, she felt "Jewish again," she said, bound by blood to the Jew Jesus. Accordingly, she went to her death as both Catholic and Jew. As Pope John Paul II said at her beatification ceremony: "In the extermination camp she died as a daughter of Israel 'for the glory of the Most Holy Name' and, at the same time, as Sister

Teresa Benedicta of the Cross, literally, 'blessed by the cross.'"

Edith was canonized in 1998, but questions raised by her canonization will always be pertinent. For example, how did the historic anti-Semitism of the Christian churches contribute to the Holocaust? And while it is true that many Christians rescued Jews, why was there any need for heroic rescues in the first place? What motivated a supposedly Christian nation to think it was acceptable to slaughter people who were different from themselves? How could the churches have failed so spectacularly to educate their followers in the truth? What are religious leaders doing today to counter prejudice and similar evils?

In this respect, Edith Stein's story has something for everyone: Jew, Muslim, Christian, Hindu—all people, everywhere.

The life of Edith Stein cannot, by itself, address all these issues. But it can open the door to deeper reflection. "My only prayer was a search for the truth," Edith said when she gave up her faith as a teenager. Eventually, she found her way to that truth and allowed the encounter to transform her. Her story might help others do the same.

ONE

The Road to the Future

Yom Kippur, the Day of Atonement, is the most solemn and widely observed feast in the Jewish calendar. The day is devoted to strict fasting and lengthy prayer. The prayer is centered on repentance before God for sin.

In 1891, this feast fell on October 12. On that day, Edith Stein was born into a Jewish family in what was then Breslau, Germany (now Wroclaw, Poland). Edith's mother, Auguste, was quite impressed by this happenstance. In fact, even though she always celebrated Edith's birthday on October 12, she always considered Yom Kippur—on whatever date it fell in later years—to be the actual birthday of her youngest child.

Had Auguste been able to peer into the future, she might have had second thoughts. Certainly she would have been devastated to see how the notion of atonement—suffering endured in reparation for sin—worked out in Edith's Christian life. Most likely, she would have been tempted to overlook the juxtaposition of her daughter's birth with the holy day.

Auguste instead laid great stress on it. Nearly fifty years later, on the eve of World War II, that early portent unfolded. In imitation of the redemptive action of Christ, Edith consciously offered herself as "a sacrifice of atonement for true peace, that if possible the reign of antichrist

13

might be broken." Her offering, as a Christian and Carmelite nun, became a reality at Auschwitz.

Auguste: A Hard Act to Follow

Edith's instinct to offer her life for others had its roots in the example of her own mother. "All light and warmth in our home came from her," Edith said.[1] This is an especially touching tribute given that Auguste, who owned and operated a lumberyard, had limited time with her family.

Further, Auguste was a single parent of seven children left with barely any resources when her husband died in 1893. At the time, Auguste was almost forty-four. Her oldest child, Paul, was twenty-one; Edith, the youngest, was nearly two.

Edith saw her father, Siegfried, for the last time the day he left for the business trip that would end in his death. She was in her mother's arms, and her father had already said good-bye and was headed out the door. Edith called him back for what proved to be a final farewell.

Shortly after, on a hot July day, Siegfried set out on a hike to inspect a forest for timber for the family's ailing lumber business. A mailman noticed him lying down and assumed he was resting. Hours later, the man passed by the place again, saw that Siegfried hadn't moved, and discovered he was dead. The probable cause was heatstroke.

Auguste's extended family descended upon the home after the funeral (cousins, aunts, and uncles are a constant theme in accounts of Stein family life). The council met and rendered their decision: She must sell the failing business, move to larger quarters, and rent out rooms to boarders.

Auguste quietly took in the proceedings, allowing herself, once, to exchange "a very expressive" look with Else, her seventeen-year-old daughter. Maybe she was sizing Else up for the task ahead. Then Auguste rendered *her* decision: She would learn the trade, get the lumberyard back on its feet, and clear up her debts. Else and others would run the household and help her care for the five younger children: Arno, Frieda, Rosa, Erna, and Edith.

Remarkably, this is what happened. As time went by and the company prospered, Auguste might even have wondered why Siegfried had been unable to make a go of things. But then, Auguste had a flair for commerce.

She was the daughter of merchants, having helped in the family grocery store from the time she was only four years old. Later, when new employees joined her parents' ever-expanding enterprise, she taught them the ropes. All that early training now paid off. She had a gift for numbers, could spot a business opportunity in the bud, had the courage to act, possessed the discernment not to overextend, and genuinely enjoyed helping people.

Years later, a friend told the family about a conversation she had overheard on a streetcar. Some men were discussing the lumber business when one declared emphatically that the best merchant in the trade in all Breslau was "Frau Stein."

But it was very hard work. Auguste was up at 5:30 every morning and out in the open most of the day. She showed customers her stock, rang up the bill, and even helped push the wagons, loaded with lumber, out through the gates. When a delivery wagon needed to be unloaded quickly, she was in the thick of it, racing the others to pass down the boards.

Auguste kept her hands firmly in the business even though she had employees and even after her son, Arno, joined her in the venture. When she was seventy, the family urged her to retire, but when she reached her eighties, Edith said, "it never even occurred to anyone anymore to suggest retirement." Given this pace, it's not surprising that Auguste often said upon retiring at night, "My bed is the most wonderful place in the world."

As a devout Jew, Auguste knew she didn't do all this entirely through her own strength. Once, after the teenage Edith had renounced belief in God, her mother countered with her own proof of his existence: "After all," she told her daughter, "I can't imagine that I owe everything I've achieved to my own ability."

Auguste supported her family more than adequately through this heroic regimen. She refused to take advantage of anything that smacked of public assistance. When her three youngest children attended the same school, tuition was waived for the third. "My mother would not avail herself of that dispensation," Edith said.

A Sunny Childhood

For many years, the family lived in a three-room apartment and the two youngest girls, Edith and Erna, shared their mother's bed. On occasion, Auguste rented out the parlor to a student. Cramped as it was, the great advantage of this apartment on Jagerstrasse was that it backed up to the family's lumberyard.

In a child-care arrangement that would land Auguste in court today, she often left Erna and Edith, preschoolers, alone in the apartment while she worked. If any problem arose, they were to call to their mother from the back window. The arrangement succeeded, Edith said, because the girls were very conscientious: "[We] would have done something we had been forbidden to do more readily in mother's presence than in her absence."

Actually, the Stein children as well as neighborhood friends and young cousins all spent a good deal of time playing at the lumberyard. Decades later, one of those cousins said: "Amongst all our friends the story went, 'Nowhere can you have so much fun playing as at the Steins,' and they gathered at our place every free afternoon."

Edith described it as a "paradise" for children. Seesaw, the simplest of their games since it involved nothing more than a board and a sawhorse, occupied them for hours. But hide-and-go-seek, she said, "was also superb." Auguste, who welcomed all this youthful activity, allowed the children to build little houses from scraps of wood. Occasionally, they picked strawberries in the large garden she kept in a corner of the lumberyard.

Edith knew that most of the credit for this sunny childhood went to her mother. Her gratitude ran deep. In fact, Edith maintained such reverence for Auguste that even as an adult, she sacrificed her own desires to her mother's emotional well-being.

When Edith was baptized in 1922, for example, she deferred her entry into the convent in large part because of the possible effect on Auguste. "When I saw my mother for the first time after [my] baptism," she later recalled, "I realized that she couldn't handle another blow for the present. Not that it would have killed her—but I couldn't have held myself responsible for the embitterment it would have caused."[2]

Nevertheless, Edith's mother was not her confidante—"no more so than anyone else," Edith observed. She had embarked in early childhood on an inner, solitary journey, and even though she had countless friends and, later, deft spiritual advisors, Edith relied in great measure on her own internal compass.

Tiny But Tough

"[As a child] I was small and frail, and despite all the care given me, always pale," Edith wrote in her autobiography, *Life in a Jewish Family*. Maybe her delicate appearance influenced her siblings, all of whom were completely devoted to her. Paul, her oldest brother, nicknamed her "Pussycat." This was either because her brothers liked to play with her "as with a kitten," she said, or because of her agility: The older children could never pin her down when they roughhoused.

It was Paul who taught her the names of the German classical poets and familiarized her with German literature. He also carried her around on his shoulders while singing student songs. Arno, when he was twenty-two, taught her to dance and "was so tall that he had to bend over quite a bit" to accommodate the seven-year-old. "This, however, bothered neither of the partners," she said. Else and Frieda were like second mothers, and Rosa, on their errands in town, treated her to apple cake and ice cream. Altogether, Edith admitted, she grew up in a cocoon.

Not that she was an entirely pleasant child. "The earliest memory I have ... [is] standing before a big white door, drumming on it with clenched fists and screaming because my elder sister was on the other side and I wanted to go to her." By nature, Edith was lively, stubborn, and easily angered if crossed: "Always in motion," she said of herself, "spilling over with pranks, impertinent and precocious."

Temper tantrums were part of her repertoire. Her sister Else, charged with keeping her siblings in line, occasionally reached the end of her rope and locked Edith in a room. Edith tried to fend off this dreaded punishment by throwing herself on the floor and becoming rigid so that Else could barely lift her. Once imprisoned, Edith screamed at the top of her lungs and pounded the floor until released.

She moderated this approach when the time came for her to go to kindergarten, but the same strong will asserted itself. Erna, her sister and soul mate, was only a year and a half older than Edith. She started first grade when the time came, leaving Edith behind with no companionship. Edith considered kindergarten "beneath her dignity," but Auguste registered her anyway.

Edith mounted a campaign of resistance. She fought with her siblings as they took turns, each day, walking her to school. To drive her point home, she was unpleasant to her classmates and refused to play.

Finally, as her sixth birthday approached, she determined "to make an end of the despised attendance at kindergarten." She begged her mother to allow her to go to the "big school" as her birthday present. Her birthday fell in October, the school year began in the spring, and Edith was well behind the older children. However, Else, who had recently completed teacher training, vouched for her younger sister's precocious intelligence and managed to secure the placement.

Edith could neither read nor write and at first found it very difficult to use a pen and read whole words. By Easter she had caught up with her classmates. After that, she said in a statement that defined her lifelong inclination, "I always maintained my place among the best students."

A Hidden World

Despite the stormy scenes, Edith felt that within her there was a "hidden world." But not an entirely cheery one. If someone mentioned a murder, the little girl would be unable to sleep, "dark horror" oppressing her. If she saw a drunkard, the sight would haunt her for days. Her mother once used a mildly offensive expression over some very minor incident, but Edith could never forget it. She was thoughtful and overly sensitive, but endured her hidden suffering silently.

"Gradually my inner world grew lighter and clearer," she said, starting with a personal transformation at the age of seven. The once-petulant child became docile and decided that her mother and Frieda, the sister currently running the household, knew what was best for her. Later, she could think of no external explanation for this shift: "I cannot explain it otherwise than that reason assumed command within me."

She did offer a secondary explanation for her transformation, one more revealing than the simple descent of reason. Edith experienced "distaste and shame" when she witnessed the rage of others: "The price of such self-indulgence was the loss of one's dignity," she said.

That price was too high for Edith. For her, personal dignity and inner freedom were paramount, so much so that as an adult she abstained from alcohol so as to lose neither of them. The self-discipline and iron will that emerged in childhood stayed with her for life.

But Edith was by no means a prig. The lumberyard camaraderie of childhood evolved as she grew, and Edith recounts, for example, tramping through town with university friends, singing student songs at the top of their lungs. Frequently, as an older student, she and her friends took mini-vacations, hiking for days through the German countryside.

When the very young and obstinate Edith fought for an academic foothold, she couldn't have understood the depth of her intellectual gifts. But she might have sensed that school was the road to her future. In a sense it turned out to *be* her future for nearly the rest of her life. She was almost more at home in school than in her own house, she said of her childhood years. At home, when she was young, the adults laughed at her precocious attempts at weighty conversation. At school, she was taken seriously.

TWO

WANDERING OFF THE PATH

O h, for once, let me be right!" a frustrated classmate once exclaimed to Edith. The two were only elementary school students at the time, but the plea is a fair measure of Edith's academic stature during those years. She admits she was an overeager student. Her contributions to class discussions were sometimes beyond the understanding of her peers.

Worse, she occasionally jumped in front of the teacher's desk, hand raised, to be sure she had a turn. But she avoided the usual retaliatory measures directed against eggheads, in part because she was modest and unassuming about her abilities. Also, she was always ready to coach the others when they needed academic help.

Sometimes her teachers unwittingly threatened to undo this fine balance. When she was a teenager, for example, a teacher told his class that "Fräulein Stein" came first in academic achievement, followed by "a big gap," after which came everybody else. Naturally, she resented this sort of remark, fearing it might disrupt the friendships she enjoyed with her classmates. They liked and trusted her, however, and found little reason to resent her.

Edith's academic success made it all the more astonishing when, in 1906, at the age of fourteen, she dropped out of school. In the German educational system of the time, students of her caliber would normally have been switching to the equivalent of high school and preparation for university studies. Her principal was disgusted by what he saw as a waste of talent.

Edith's reasoning: "I had been sitting on a school bench long enough." A slight dip in her academic performance had troubled her. Also, she found herself preoccupied with what she called "ideological questions" that were not addressed in the school curriculum. (She did not identify these.) Further complicating these adjustments were the physical changes that were taking place as she matured.

She wanted a break, although this looked more like a departure: She was leaving school without addressing the possibility of return. Her mother, who had confidence in Edith's judgment, didn't try to influence her one way or the other.

And so the budding intellectual became a mother's helper.

Life in the Slow Lane

Within weeks of dropping out of school, Edith moved to Hamburg for six weeks to assist her now-married sister, Else. The always-frail Else, mother of an eighteen-month-old daughter, was in the final weeks of a difficult second pregnancy.

Edith was and always remained fairly inept when it came to domestic chores. Nevertheless, she took to her new responsibilities with the kind of goodwill that can lead to a great deal of success. When the new mother was back on her feet and occasionally out of the house for the morning, Edith not only took care of the children and the housework; she also fixed her brother-in-law's lunch. It was ready and waiting when Max stopped in at noon.

Else, who had helped raise Edith and loved her as intensely as she loved her own children, couldn't bring herself to send her sister home. Ten months went by before Auguste, anxious not to alienate Else, finally summoned Edith back to Breslau.

She might have done so sooner had she realized the effect on Edith of life in Else and Max's home. The young couple had no religious faith, and Edith heard many conversations that undermined her own beliefs. Her brother-in-law was a doctor, and she read his books as avidly as she read any others. He specialized in dermatology and blood disorders, including the treatment of syphilis. She later concluded, too late, that these books were not suitable for a teenage girl.

The net effect was that Edith, while in Hamburg, gave up her faith and made a deliberate decision to stop praying, embarking instead on a "search for the truth." She still felt she was destined for a great future, but she had no idea what that might be or how she would get there.

Her search for the truth was a legitimate quest, though. Edith never used her loss of faith as an excuse for self-indulgence. Even without the motivation of religion, she detested the loose morals of the time and guarded her own chastity.

On the other hand, having become an attractive young woman during the stay in Hamburg, she was no longer, she said, the completely "innocent child." She was pleased when she discovered in her friendships with several men that she didn't always have to use words to get what she wanted. She could achieve the desired result with "a single glance."

In the long run, her turning away from prayer marked the paradoxical beginning of a turning to God. It would be many years, though, before Edith reached that conclusion.

Getting Up to Speed

Back in Breslau in the spring of 1907, Edith was adrift. Pleasantly so, for the most part. She spent a lot of time reading, especially the works of Shakespeare. She played tennis, rowed, and hiked.

She seemed most galvanized, however, by the academic challenges of her sister, Erna, who was a high school student. Erna had set her sights on becoming a physician, so she had a formidable amount of work to cover. Edith made Erna's cause her own.

Edith was the one to prod and question and direct Erna each time she had to write an essay. Sometimes Edith wrote the introductions to Erna's compositions. Once, she wrote the entire essay when Erna's failed to meet her standards. Erna turned it in to the teacher. On no occasion did the question of cheating seem to have occurred to them.

And still Edith drifted. She had missed her opportunity to proceed to higher studies, and though the idea still appealed to her, she felt she couldn't make up the work. Her brothers and sisters suggested various options—art school, photography—which she rejected. Only her mother, for the moment, prudently said nothing.

One morning, as the summer wound down, Auguste sat with Edith and brushed her hair, a ritual she enjoyed and Edith happily permitted even though the fifteen-year-old could easily do it herself. At last, Auguste broached the topic, and Edith admitted that she regretted leaving school. Auguste dismissed the notion that school was no longer a viable choice. Within a few days, in fact, she had worked up a plan of action.

Richard Courant, a cousin and gifted mathematician, stopped by shortly after this conversation to visit his Aunt Auguste. She set the problem before him. Courant had long admired his cousin's exceptional intelligence. Edith could make up the work and prepare for entrance exams within a year, he said. He himself would teach her math. Courant recruited a fellow scholar to teach Latin. The project was soon underway.

Edith made such remarkable progress that she later identified this time of intense academic work as the first entirely happy period of her life. She attributed this situation to the opportunity to use her intellect at full throttle. She liked math well enough—she thought of it as mental gymnastics—and whistled a few triumphant bars of music each time she solved a problem.

However, when her cousin moved away to accept a position at the University in Göttingen, Edith's new tutor proved far less able. Her sense of urgency irritated him. She was so extraordinarily gifted, he complained, that she had already made exceptional progress. Why did she demand more?

Latin, on the other hand, "was something else again." She later wrote: "It was as though I were learning my mother tongue." The strict rules of Latin grammar challenged her. She could and did translate with skill. Her tutor pushed her without mercy. In the end he was able to tell her she had a more proficient and accurate command of Latin grammar than just about anyone he knew.

Edith reviewed French, English, and history on her own. In six months, half the time her cousin had predicted, she was ready for her exams. Her mother, quietly supportive, dropped by the school on exam day to await the results with her nervous daughter. Erna came, too. In the afternoon, the principal read out the names of those who had passed for the various levels. Edith, one of three candidates for her level, was the only one of the three accepted.

She never regretted those two years away from the stress of

academic life. Now physically strong and mentally primed, the sixteen-year-old dropout reentered school in the spring of 1908.

School Matters

Edith's decision to go back to school wasn't the foregone conclusion it seems in retrospect. She herself let the issue coast until moved by an "inner compulsion." She couldn't figure out where her decisions came from, she said, floating up, as they did, from some unfathomable depth.

Once an idea took hold, though, Edith ran with it. All the better, too, if the idea seemed impossible. She played out such moments as if engaged in a game.

The decision to reenter, and the subsequent work that entailed, were a bigger challenge than the actual work once she got there. She was diligent, though, and received her usual excellent grades, literally jumping for joy whenever her essays received a perfect score. "I keep thinking you ought to be used to it by now," a classmate once remarked.

The students were a tight-knit group. Edith particularly admired a friend named Hedi, who was exceptionally talented but so modest, Edith said, that "despite her achievements, she never gained a reputation for being a brilliant student." Edith, of course, did gain that reputation, and along with it, something less pleasant. Occasionally, she came across as arrogant or as at least insensitive to the feelings of others. "Don't be so forward," an exasperated classmate remarked once when Edith spoke up in class. The teacher quietly agreed.

On another occasion, the class decided to play a game while returning on the train from a trip. "Forfeits" required that a student leave the compartment while the others discussed her good and bad points. Then they made a list and asked the victim in question to guess who had mentioned each characteristic.

This is the sort of pastime that can lead to hurt feelings, but the teacher not only permitted it, he joined in. All went well during Edith's turn until the students read out their teacher's remark: Edith was inclined to gloat over the troubles of others. Hedi nodded in agreement.

Edith, horrified, burst into tears. Her classmates' efforts to console her hardly made things better. The teacher probably had that impression, they said, because she tended to laugh "at some of the dumb answers given in class."

In spite of her shortcomings, Edith was a leader and trusted friend. Besides, she was clever enough to outsmart the administration, always a boon in the high school years. She proved her skill in this regard during her final year when she hatched a plan to avoid attending the dreaded Sedan Day celebration.

This patriotic annual event marked the triumph of the Germans over the French at Sedan in 1870. The conservative underpinnings of the day irritated the politically liberal Edith. Also, although she was thoroughly patriotic, she thought it mean-spirited to disparage the French so many years after the defeat. Nevertheless, the entire school was required to attend and celebrate with speeches, songs, and poems.

Edith refused to participate but had to think of a plausible excuse. With the approval of her classmates, she proposed to the principal that they be allowed to take Sedan Day and the following day for a class trip, their last opportunity before graduation. He agreed but attached a condition: They had to observe Sedan Day en route. This meant a speech, a task that naturally fell to Edith.

She wrote one in verse which, she said later, "substantially differed from the usual speeches." Her method of delivery sheds a little light on that cryptic remark. One of the girls had brought along a puppet designed to resemble a Chinese man. The puppet delivered the address.

One Door Closes, Another Opens

Final exams took place in the spring of 1911, and Edith did so well that she was exempt from the oral phase of the tests. At home, the family set out a torte with their congratulations spelled out on top in chocolate letters. Auguste tied up the phone calling Edith's aunts and uncles to report the good news and putting Edith on the line to accept their congratulations.

The evening passed in a buzz of excitement, so Edith was all the more puzzled when she awoke the next day feeling an unexpected letdown. She stayed in bed a little longer, mulling over her inner sense of emptiness. "A beloved and familiar way of life was gone forever," she later wrote, and she was momentarily uncertain of the future—particularly of her decision to study such subjects as Latin and philosophy at the university.

Philosophy especially seemed completely impractical, with little hope of financial reward. And Edith did need to earn her living. But while other family members were distressed by the young woman's academic choices, her mother shielded the scholar from interference.

Auguste once suggested that Edith study law. Since women were not yet admitted to the bar, that suggestion was easily disposed of. It is a measure of how well she knew her daughter that she never mentioned professions such as nursing or counseling. "Do whatever you think is right for you," she told Edith firmly.

As Edith lay in bed that morning debating her future, she put the matter to rest. "We are in the world to serve humanity," she reasoned. "This is best accomplished when doing that for which one has the requisite talents.... Therefore ... the conclusion seemed to me to be indisputable."

She shrugged off her doubts. She had the requisite talents for abstract thinking and an interest in teaching. Each of these interests could support the other. Edith would put her hand to it and see where her path led.

THREE

A Family Like Any Other

While Edith negotiated a path to her future, Auguste provided a home base for her expanding clan. She liked to have as many of her children living with her as she could, even after they married. In 1910, when Edith was nearly finished with high school, Auguste bought the substantial house that made this possible.

Seventy percent of the buildings in Breslau were destroyed during World War II, but the Stein home still stands. Although Edith lived here only a few years, she returned for vacations, family visits, and several extended stays. It was from this home that she left for the Carmelite convent in 1933, and it was here that her mother died in 1936.

The building, now owned by the Edith Stein Society of Wroclaw, is dedicated to Stein's life and to Polish-German and Christian-Jewish dialogue. In its sheer size and magnificence, though, it is a silent testimony to Auguste herself and to the strength of Jewish family life in early twentieth-century Germany.

Jewish family life, it turns out, was very much like any other family life.

Edith's autobiography, *Life in a Jewish Family*, covers the years to 1916. Those years in her family—and beyond—teemed with relatives, marriages, divorce, death, births, business, and education.

In the house on Michaelisstrasse, many of these threads came together under one elegant roof. The vast banquet room on the second floor, featuring inlaid parquet floors and four huge windows, easily held Erna's grand piano as well as an enormous dining table. An adjoining smoking room was nearly as large and equally elegant. Still, there was plenty of room for bedrooms and a large bathroom.

The kitchen and dining room were on the ground floor. Next to them was office space for Erna when she completed her medical studies and set up a practice in obstetrics and gynecology.

In addition, the house was divided vertically although unequally, so that a smaller section served as a separate living area, much like a duplex today. For many years, Arno, his wife Martha, and their four children lived in that unit.

Over the years, the house was also home to Erna; her husband, Hans; their two children, Susanne and Ernest; Hans' mother, Dorothea; Auguste; her daughters Rosa, Edith, and Frieda; Frieda's daughter, Erika; Auguste's two sisters, Mika and Clara; as well as assorted friends who, from time to time, needed a home.

In-Laws and Other Aggravations

It wasn't always easy. Sometimes, Auguste herself was part of the problem. She was a critical and demanding mother-in-law—"a poor mother-in-law," her daughters flatly stated, only half in jest. Her son Paul, for example, became engaged and tried for years to win his mother's approval of his fiancée, Trude. For reasons of her own, Auguste refused her blessing, relenting only when the couple finally married.

Auguste probably sensed from the start that Trude's free-spirited approach to life would result in messy housekeeping and casual parenting. True to her mother-in-law's expectations, Trude, a milliner and musician, kept a cluttered home, even raising canaries in the kitchen. Every visit there, Edith said, cost Auguste "a tremendous amount of self-control." She refused to drink Trude's coffee, and rather than eat any cake she might supply, Auguste brought along on her visits Rosa's homemade *Streuselkuchen*.

Edith later wrote affectionately of her brother Paul, who shared her interests in the theater and music. Like her, he was "a passionate bookworm." As she grew older, however, she never acted as a mediator between Auguste and her brother, as she sometimes did between her mother and other family members. Paul was old enough to be her father, after all, but he was also so quiet and easygoing that he rarely clashed with anyone.

Edith did stay in touch with him—as she did all her relatives—even after she entered Carmel. Not long before her own death, she wrote anxiously to a friend about Paul and Trude's precarious existence in Breslau under the Nazis. They expected to be turned out of their home any day, she said. "So far, all attempts by our relatives in America to get them over there have been in vain. They report the facts without complaint." (Paul and Trude were deported to the Theresienstadt concentration camp in 1942 and died there in 1943.)

In contrast to her attitude toward Paul and Trude, Auguste heartily approved of Arno's marriage to Martha. It wasn't long, however, before she could barely suppress her irritation over Martha's sloppy housekeeping. Auguste was a businesswoman, used to running a tight ship both at work and at home. Martha was lively, funny, and full of anecdotes, and she loved to spend her days shopping and visiting.

Worse, since they lived in the same house, Auguste had every opportunity to observe Martha's nonchalant child-rearing efforts.

Arno and Martha's daughter, Eva, for example, was retarded. Auguste was convinced that Martha neglected the girl, so she herself taught Eva how to eat properly, talk, and do many of the small tasks of everyday life.

Martha and Arno's children thrived, in spite of Auguste's misgivings, and bonded easily with the other cousins living under their grandmother's roof. These formed a cheerful band, relatively unaware of adult friction. Edith, who had exceptional rapport with children, enjoyed their company.

She happened to be home for an extended stay in 1920, for example, just when Arno's son, Helmut, was recovering from the flu. He was confined to bed in a room off Edith's study, from which he clamored for her attention. Finally, she brought her work in and sat at a desk near his bed, attempting to write.

This wasn't good enough for Helmut, who demanded that she entertain him. If he didn't stop badgering her, she told him, she wouldn't be able to work.

"Well, you don't have to," he replied.

"And that was so convincing," Edith said, "that I went to play with him."

Edith's affection for children mirrored her mother's. Auguste had a "vibrant *joie de vivre* [and] unflappable sense of humor," her granddaughter Susanne said in her memoir *Aunt Edith*. Auguste was in her element with her grandchildren.

Even into her seventies, she would bathe the young ones, regaling them with show tunes. Then she would wrap them in huge towels and dry them off while pretending they were piles of dough that she was kneading for bread. "That proceeded with lots of tickling and pinching until we were totally out of breath with laughter," her grandson Ernest said, "Grandmother no less than we."[1]

Despite the tensions, Auguste's relationship with Arno and Martha rolled along rather uneventfully for a few years. Gradually, however, she began to suspect that Martha was trying to finagle greater financial control of the lumberyard on Arno's behalf, but to the detriment of his sisters. These women would need to rely on income from the business when Auguste passed away. So Auguste decided to develop a business plan and put it in writing.

Auguste, who had come to rely on Edith's skill as a negotiator, turned to her youngest daughter for help. Arno had a hot temper that intimidated everyone but Edith. Would she mind telling him about the plan?

Auguste and her daughters came before him presenting a united front. As they expected, he was hurt, but with the calm Edith in charge, he didn't fly off the handle. He did, however, request a mediator other than his youngest sister. A trusted uncle stepped in to draw up the settlement that made Arno a partner in the business yet protected the financial interests of his sisters.

Martha, in fact, may never have had any designs on the family business. Edith glosses over the possibility in her autobiography. She does make the point that Auguste and her children, as a unit, offered a daunting facade.

"The family's strong individual cast posed a formidable obstacle to its assimilating any alien elements," she said. Auguste concurred. Of those who didn't meet her expectations, she said resignedly, "They are altogether different from us."

The Ties That Bind

Some members of Edith's family relied on her peacemaking ability more than others. The childhood bond between Edith and her sister Erna, for example, often brought Erna to her for advice. This was especially true when Erna became engaged in 1918 to Hans Biberstein, a fellow doctor. (Edith, who met Hans first, was attracted to him, but his affection settled on Erna. Edith yielded gracefully but remained his lifelong friend.)

Tensions soon erupted between Auguste, Hans, and Hans' mother, Dorothea, who was in poor health and wanted to live with the couple after they married. Hans, who was devoted to his widowed mother, strongly encouraged her plans. Dorothea was a difficult woman, however, and Auguste wanted to spare her daughter this fate. In the heat of the moment, Auguste sometimes failed to weigh her words when talking with Hans and Dorothea. The relationship deteriorated on all sides.

Erna, caught in the middle, frequently came to Edith, saying, "I don't know what to do; I'm desperate." Edith listened, soothed, advised when asked, and generally recommended that Erna "give in, in all that is not unjust." Convinced that Hans and Erna were "meant for each other," she was sure that the intimacy of marriage would smooth out the conflict.

Eventually, it became clear that Dorothea would have to stay in her own apartment. There was a housing shortage at the time, and no place big enough for the three could be found. Hans and Erna moved into the attic on Michaelisstrasse, and the situation quieted down. (To her credit, Auguste welcomed Dorothea into her home on Michaelisstrasse eight years later when Arno and Martha moved out and space became available.)

Even Else, fifteen years older than Edith, relied on her sister for advice. Else was worn out by the births of three children in close succession and unable to muster the strength to raise them properly. Nor did she have the energy to maintain her household.

The medical practice of her husband Max was in decline, largely due to the introduction of health insurance in Germany, a movement he opposed. In 1914, Max left his wife and ordered Auguste to come to Hamburg to take her daughter home. When they got Max's letter, Edith recalled, the family sat around the dining table after lunch, deeply depressed, discussing the situation. To spare her mother the strain, Edith volunteered to go to Hamburg to talk with the couple.

Once there, she found herself listening on the one hand to all the complaints and bitterness that Max had accumulated over the years. On the other hand, Else insisted on dredging up in great and embarrassing detail all the complications of her married life. She talked incessantly. "There was no escape from it, even at night," Edith said. She worked out an agreement that entailed bringing Else home to recuperate, get medical care, and generally pull herself together. The couple eventually reunited, and both of them, Edith said, became calmer with advancing age.

Edith was not called upon to intervene when her sister Frieda's brief arranged marriage broke up. Frieda simply moved into Michaelisstrasse with her infant daughter, Erika, and quietly resumed her work as bookkeeper for the family business. But maybe Edith's exposure to the complications of married life influenced her to reflect, years later, that consecrated virginity is more radical but possibly easier than marriage.

In spite of their difficulties, Edith's family stuck together, helped each other, and never let hard times swamp the general goodwill. And they knew how to celebrate. When Erna and Hans married in 1920, for example, so many guests were invited that the reception had to be held as separate parties over two days. The dinner after the wedding, limited to the "intimate circle" of the immediate family, still ran to fifty people. Edith—who had a knack for comedy—wrote a humorous play in the couple's honor, which three cousins presented for the crowd. Other events—Auguste's eightieth birthday party, New Year's Day, family birthdays, end-of-summer celebrations—also received careful and happy attention.

Altogether, life in a Jewish family was no different from life in any other family, and that was the point of Edith's book. She started *Life in a Jewish Family* in 1933, at the suggestion of a priest, to counteract the anti-Semitic rhetoric of the Nazi movement. She never finished it, however, and in any event, the book was only published posthumously, after the War.

Although it never got to serve the purpose she and her priest friend had in mind, the book has nevertheless given the world an unusually rich source for information about Edith herself, always set within the context of her thriving family. Even when, at nineteen, she began study at the University of Breslau, she didn't depart from home. Edith lived with her family for two more years, blending an intense student life with life on Michaelisstrasse.

FOUR

THE SEEKER OF TRUTH

Perhaps it was the pace of life on Michaelisstrasse that left Edith with little patience for deadweights. At any rate, within a few days of setting foot on campus at the University of Breslau, she had sized up the student body well enough to conclude that she was surrounded by slackers. She privately dubbed most of them "The Idiots."

She wouldn't even look at them in the lecture rooms. Most of them, Edith thought, fell into the usual academic black holes of apathy, excessive partying, or career anxiety. "The mass of students I considered a negligible quantity," she said, and never found reason to modify her opinion in her two years there.

She did have likeminded friends among the students lucky enough to escape her blanket disapproval. These included her sister Erna and Hans Biberstein. But it was clear that Edith could be less than tolerant. She didn't seem to realize, either, how critical of others she had become, much less how unappealing some contemporaries might find this side of her personality.

Some found her "enchantingly malicious," she said, but Hugo Hermsen, a fellow student, set her straight. When her studies at Breslau were almost over, Edith prepared to leave for further work at the University of Göttingen. Hermsen wished her well. At the same time, with a bluntness to match her own, he told her that he hoped she would find in Göttingen people more to her taste. "Here," he added, "you seem to have become far too critical."

As mild as this remark was, it shocked Edith. She was not used to criticism from her family. "At home, hardly anyone dared to criticize me," she said. Nor did she hear it from her loving and admiring friends.

"I had been living in the naïve conviction that I was perfect," she went on. And then, with a dawning of the spiritual insight that was to accelerate and deepen:

> This is frequently the case with persons without any faith who live an exalted ethical idealism. Because one is enthused about what is good, one believes oneself to be good. I had always considered it my privilege to make remarks about everything I found negative, inexorably pointing out other people's weaknesses, mistakes, or faults of which I became aware, often using a ridiculing or sarcastic tone of voice.

Edith wasn't angry with Hermsen. On the contrary, she knew she deserved his frank critique. She seems to have been already moving toward a maturity that let her accept Hermsen's wake-up call. It was, she said, "a first alert to which I gave much reflection."[1]

Swimming in Sunshine

But not even "The Idiots" could dampen Edith's enthusiasm for the academic life. She would have taken forty hours of classes that first semester at Breslau except that she ran into too many scheduling conflicts. As it was, her full schedule left her swimming "in delight as a fish does in clear water and warm sunshine."

While she thought of herself as a seeker of knowledge, unfettered by practical considerations, she knew her family expected a more pragmatic return. At the end of her studies, she must be able to make a living. To that end, Edith needed classes that would qualify her to take the state board exams for those who wanted to teach at a university level. She signed up for a variety of courses—drama, history, philosophy, psychology—but in the end, it was the psychology that won her over. In fact, she decided to pursue a doctorate in that field.

Although psychology as an academic discipline was in its infancy, it's easy to see why it would appeal to Edith as a seeker of truth: The subject would afford her an opportunity to examine the essence of the human individual. One of her professors was William Stern, who developed the concept of and the means to measure the intelligence quotient (IQ). At the time, there was an effort underway to reduce psychology to a hard and quantifiable science, like chemistry. The students objected to this movement and felt Stern's work with the IQ and with occupational aptitude tests fed into it.

Unbowed by Stern's international stature or his genial nature, the students went head-to-head with him in his seminars. Edith said that as he expounded his views, sitting with his students around the U-shaped seminar table, they "would frequently respond in unison with a very decided and resounding 'No!'"

This was the sort of intellectual jousting that Edith loved. She might have wanted to find the truth, but on the way there she didn't want to miss anything. The exhilarating challenge made it inevitable that she would stick with psychology for her four semesters at the University of Breslau.

Edith spent most of her day studying, frequently alone, but she was not a loner. She even found study partners from time to time, men or women with whom she memorized Greek verb forms, for example, or did "mutual work projects." She studied Old High German with one partner and moved on to Ulfilas' translation of the Bible. "That provided my first acquaintance with the Gospel," she said, although "it had no religious impact."

Any time left over from studies Edith devoted to extracurricular activities. She joined the Pedagogical Group, an association of future teachers that had a lively social side, most evident in the students' freewheeling, late-night discussions. The university building they met in closed at 10:00 P.M., usually while they were still hotly debating the pros and cons of such issues as coeducation. (Edith was an enthusiastic proponent.) When that happened, the students adjourned to a café. Sometimes, in the summer, they moved on to Scheitniger Park, an old English garden, to hear the nightingales sing.

On her return from one of these late-night sessions, Edith had a rare clash with her mother over the propriety of Edith's behavior. A male student escorted her home—other students usually joined them—and they continued their discussion as they paced back and forth in front of her gate. Auguste was uncomfortable with the scene because it was far too similar to Else's midnight lingering. Edith sharply pointed out that Else's situation involved "admirers," whereas Edith and her cohorts had no designs on one another. Edith must have taken her mother to task rather severely, because later, Edith said, she "bitterly repented" of her harsh words.

Edith, a feminist, also worked with the Prussian Society for Women's Right to Vote. Her views on this subject had long been established. In high school, her peers had presented her with a bit of doggerel they wrote in her honor: "Let woman equal be with man / so loud this suffragette avers. / In days to come we surely can / See that a Cab'net Post is hers."

The Women's Student Union, however, provided her with the social outlet she needed as well as a place to hang out with her friends. When they sponsored a costume ball for professors and students at the end of the year, Edith, an excellent dancer, danced till 6:00 in the morning. She still had the stamina, on the walk home, to pursue a heated philosophical discussion with a friend.

Generous by nature, Edith wanted to give back some of what she received. When invited to help out with the Humboldt Society for Adult Education, she was on board immediately. When an unexpected opportunity presented itself, she lost no time quietly putting her feminist convictions to the test.

Two male university students needed a third student to help teach three upcoming classes for the Society. Edith agreed to help, only to find out later from a friend that the two men took advantage of their position to pursue the women in their classes. These somewhat older working women, unsure of themselves, suffered at their hands.

Without letting on she had inside knowledge, Edith suggested to the two that she teach the women while they teach the men. Seeing no reasonable objection and unable to acknowledge their lecherous intentions, they agreed. They regrouped, however. Right before the first session began, they surprised her with a decision of their own: They preferred to teach mixed classes.

Edith calmly suggested that they give the students a choice. Cornered, the two agreed, and all but one woman chose to go with Edith. The grateful women, at the end of the semester, gave Edith a bouquet of roses and a book of art history, and they even wrote to her after her studies at Breslau ended.

Her work with the Humboldt Society was as a volunteer, but Edith also tutored students from her old high school for a fee. She gave the money she earned to her mother, who put it back into the business and credited it to Edith. Auguste, ever the businesswoman, had set up individual accounts in the family company for her children.

These accounts grew along with the business and eventually ran to about $2,500 each, a hefty sum in those days. Edith met her expenses from that fund. Later, she discovered that Auguste generously brought the account back to its original level at the end of each year.

Her busy life left Edith little time for her family. She hardly ever ate with the others and, when she did, had little to contribute to the conversation. Erna could regale them with medical stories, but Edith's abstract philosophical and psychological studies didn't lend themselves to easy discussion. The family missed her former attentiveness, but like many a twenty-year-old before and since, Edith was oblivious to much that fell outside her own concerns. "I saw myself as richly endowed and a highly privileged creature," she wrote.

That makes one particular incident from those years even more intriguing. Erna and Edith shared a bedroom and each night turned the gas lamp in their room down to a very low level, leaving a dim light burning. One morning, Frieda came to get them up, opened the door, and screamed as the odor of gas flooded out.

The lamp had flickered out, and the gas had begun to do its work. Frieda threw open a window and roused her extremely pale sisters, each in a very heavy stupor. Edith recalled how disappointed she was to be spared this "dreamless" death. She was shocked, she said, to discover that she had so little motivation to cling to life.

Looking Toward Göttingen

Edith had always intended to move on to another university for further study at some point in her academic career. The possibility presented itself late in 1912, when she wasn't actively looking. While reading essays on the psychology of thought for one of Stern's seminars, she came across frequent references to the work of the philosopher Edmund Husserl. Richard Moskiewicz, Edith's close friend and fellow student, gave her the second volume of Husserl's book, *Logical Investigations*, telling her that all the other writers she had been reading got their ideas from him.

Moskiewicz was a medical doctor now studying philosophy. He had worked under Husserl at the University of Göttingen and was nostalgic for that town where people "philosophize, day and night, at meals, in the street, everywhere." Moskiewicz told Edith about the system of thought founded by Husserl—phenomenology—which attempts to analyze the essence of all phenomena. The phenomenologist searches to the root of what a person can actually know about objects outside himself and then asks how he can know these things. This was right up Edith's alley.

The truth was that Edith was beginning to find psychology unsatisfying. Maybe it was time for her to take a closer look at philosophy. Not long after, she saw in a journal a photograph of a female student of Husserl who had won a prize for a philosophical paper. She was intrigued by the combination—a woman who was also a philosopher and a prizewinner. (Edith could not have guessed that some years down the road this philosopher, Hedwig Martius-Conrad, was destined to play a role in her conversion.)

A few days later, the wife of her cousin and former math tutor,

Richard Courant, invited her to come to Göttingen, where the young couple lived. "That put paid to all arguments," Edith said. She made plans to spend the summer semester of 1913 studying at the university there.

Her enthusiasm was evident to everyone. At the family's New Year's Eve celebration, her friends worked up verses set to popular songs for all the guests in attendance. According to Edith's chorus: "Many a maiden dreams of *busserl* [kisses] / Edith, though, of naught but Husserl. / In Göttingen she soon will see / Husserl as real as real can be."

Her mother didn't stop her from going, although Edith noted that she seemed sadder than expected over just a summer's-long separation. Perhaps she knew, subconsciously, that Edith would never really live at home again.

Edith might have suspected the same. As if to ward off that possibility, and even though her interest in psychology had begun to wane, she asked Stern to assign her a topic for a dissertation. Within a few weeks at Göttingen, however, she began to suspect that psychology would soon give way to the more satisfying field of philosophy.

FIVE

PHILOSOPHY, 24/7

One day, when Edith was still a student at the University of Breslau, she stopped in to see her former high school principal. He asked her how she was doing. Edith, who said she lived in a state of "general euphoria," responded, "Oh, *I'm* doing *very* well!"

His eyes grew wide, and he exclaimed in surprise, "Well, one seldom hears *that!*"

Things would only get better in Göttingen. For the first time in her life, Edith was completely on her own: "I was twenty-one years old and looked forward full of expectation to all that lay ahead." Since she was at Göttingen to acquaint herself with the work of Edmund Husserl, what lay immediately ahead was the philosophical universe. Edith stepped confidently in.

Adolf Reinach, a lecturer in philosophy at the university and Husserl's right-hand man, provided entrée into this world. Reinach, thirty-three years old and newly married, greeted her with such good will that Edith was taken by surprise. Only relatives and friends had ever been so warm and openhearted.

"It was like a first glimpse into a completely new world," she said. Actually, Edith's reputation had preceded her. Moskiewicz—their mutual friend—had written to Reinach about her, and he was genuinely pleased to meet her.

Adolf and his wife, Anna, were Jewish, as were many of those in the philosophical milieu Edith was entering. A number of the men and women Edith admired were converting to Christianity, however, including, a few years down the road, the Reinachs themselves. The young couple would later figure in Edith's conversion, but for now, she appreciated their warmth and intellectual integrity. As yet, Edith's search for truth was wholly secular. Slowly, at Göttingen, that would change.

But first, she had to meet "the Master," as his students called Husserl. She attended a preliminary philosophical meeting at which he talked with and accepted the newcomers, one by one. Reinach had alerted Husserl to his talented new student, and the Master was pleased when Edith told him that she had already read volume two of his complex *Logical Investigations*. "Why, that's a heroic achievement!" he said, and invited her to join his seminar.

A Vigorous Intellectual Life

At last, Edith seemed to be on track, ready for the sort of vigorous intellectual investigations that would lead her, she hoped, to the core meaning of human existence. "Mos," as Edith called Moskiewicz, had assumed she would join the Philosophical Society, a small band of Husserl's students who met weekly for discussion. She did.

At her first meeting she jumped into the debate, not realizing that generally students waited several semesters to join the Society, and then waited many months before daring to join in the discussion. Mos, the chairman of the group, ignored this unspoken protocol with Edith, as did most of the others. All, in fact, except Grete Ortmann, an older student who clearly resented the newcomer and her contributions.

Grete's enmity was so obvious that Reinach privately upbraided her for her hostile attitude toward Edith, who after all, he said, was "so nice." But she resented Edith's enthusiastic participation in every discussion anyway, especially since the subject matter was so arcane. For her part, Edith found Grete ponderous, given to making trivial statements with an air of great solemnity.

With her keen eye for telling detail, Edith was not above pointing out that this "delicate bit of a person" had such a heavy tread that "she usually splattered her coat, way up, with mud from Göttingen's streets." She remained friendly toward her opponent, though, in spite of the fact that Grete refused to draw Edith into the Society's social life. As a senior and leading female member of the group, it would have been up to Grete to do this. Under the circumstances, Grete's hostility at first limited Edith's social contacts with the Society.

She slowly made inroads, however. Edith first met Fritz Kaufmann, for example, while she was on a walk, picking violets. He had seen her at the preliminary group meeting with Husserl and now joined her for her stroll.

The elegant, wealthy Kaufmann was destined to become a lifelong friend. But Fritz came across as pretentious and conceited, so much so that Reinach, on their first meeting, nearly threw him out. ("Reinach rejected arrogance whenever he met it," Edith observed.) She saw through the surface manner and teased Kaufmann relentlessly, gradually loosening him up. Once, in a seminar, the class was "secretly delighted," Edith recalled, when an American sitting next to Kaufmann energetically shook out his pen, stirring obvious anxiety in the fastidious German over potential damage to his flawless clothing.

Hans Lipps "made a deeper impression on [her] than did anyone else." He was twenty-three, slim, well built, and handsome. He was also brilliant, studying philosophy and medicine simultaneously. All signs indicate that Edith was attracted to him and hoped for a future together.

She had always been discreet on the subject, even though she admitted to dreaming about "a great love and a happy marriage." She had at times found a young man whom she thought might fit the bill and who appealed to her as a potential husband. "But hardly anyone was aware of this," she said, because she always seemed indifferent in this regard. At any rate, the relationship never developed romantically, although she and Hans were good friends and stayed in touch for years.

An Unknown World

Edith took a heavy schedule of classes that summer, from "The Psychophysics of Visual Perception," which she enjoyed "but only in the way [she] did theoretical physics," to a course on Kant's *Critique of Practical Reason.* By far the most influential intellectual experience of the semester took place during the lectures of the phenomenologist Max Scheler. Scheler's personal life was messy at the time. He was divorced and his first wife had taken him to court, accusing him of scandalous behavior. As a result, the university refused him faculty privileges, and he could speak to the students only if they invited him privately and if they did not advertise his lectures.

Scheler was a charismatic personality with a dazzling touch as a lecturer. Whereas Husserl was dry, logical, and concerned with rigorous objectivity and "radical intellectual honesty," Scheler scattered "ingenious suggestions" around and worked with topics that were of personal interest to young people. Edith felt some sort of luminous spark flickering in him, and in fact, he had recently returned to the Catholic faith. He was "full of Catholic ideas," she said, and these had a significant though subtle effect on Edith.

"This was my first encounter with a hitherto totally unknown world," she later wrote.

> It did not as yet lead me to the faith. But it did open for me a region of "phenomena" which I could then no longer bypass blindly. With good reason we were repeatedly enjoined to observe all things without prejudice, to discard all possible "blinders." The barriers of rationalistic prejudices with which I had unwittingly grown up fell, and the world of faith unfolded before me. Persons with whom I associated daily, whom I esteemed and admired, lived in it. At the least, they deserved my giving it some serious reflection.
>
> For the time being, I did not embark on a systematic investigation of the questions of faith; I was far too busy with other matters. I was content to accept without resistance the stimuli coming from my surroundings, and so, almost without noticing it, became gradually transformed.[1]

Husserl, too, was Christian, having converted from Judaism as a younger man. Edith didn't seem especially interested in this aspect of his character. The philosopher's objectivity and his efforts, as a phenomenologist, to analyze and describe the essence of all phenomena were what absorbed her attention. Husserl did insist on the reality of the supernatural, however, and this became a factor in Edith's intellectual quest.

The class that had the greatest impact on Edith was outside the philosophy department and affected her for reasons unrelated to the class itself. She took a course on the age of absolutism and enlightenment, which required a term paper. Hers was so impressive that the professor, Max Lehmann, suggested she rework it a bit and submit it as part of the requirements for the state boards that would conclude her university studies.

Edith had intended to get her doctorate first and then take the boards sometime in the distant future. Lehmann's suggestion changed her plans. She decided to stay at Göttingen—this would enable her to revise her thesis—and get her doctorate under Husserl. In truth, she found the thought of leaving Göttingen unbearable.

She wrote to Professor Stern to confess that she had done nothing on her assignment in psychology. Instead, she told him, she now wished to pursue a doctorate in philosophy. He encouraged her to do so. Edith then approached Husserl to discuss a doctoral theme.

Husserl was taken by surprise: People usually requested a thesis only after years of study. He discussed the enormous amount of work involved in producing a dissertation and told her to take the state boards first. But then, when she still seemed determined, he relented.

Edith proposed the notion of empathy as her topic. This would allow her to explore a subject of growing interest to her, the psycho-physical-spiritual nature of what it means to be a person in relation to other persons. Husserl had indirectly suggested the idea in his seminar that summer. "An objective outer world can only be experienced inter-subjectively," he had said, through individuals who interact. Accordingly, "an experience of other individuals is a prerequisite."

Husserl called this experience "empathy." Another philosopher, Theodor Lipps (no relation to Hans Lipps), had described the experience but had not defined it. Edith wanted to take a shot at examining what empathy might mean.

Husserl liked the topic but imposed a heavy burden: She must analyze the many works of Theodore Lipps as the starting point of her dissertation. Edith found this a "bitter pill" but immediately started to make plans. She would get the state boards "off [her] back as soon as possible" and get the outline of her dissertation together over the winter. "This then," she said, "was the result of my first summer in Göttingen."

SIX

DESPAIR AND THE ACADEMIC

When Edith returned home at the end of the semester, it was almost as if she had never left. Her friends welcomed her back into their social life. She was an academic success, and they applauded her for it, but she was still "one of them."

Auguste, supportive as usual, gave her the go-ahead to pursue her studies at Göttingen. Even Professor Stern jumped on the bandwagon. He continued to include her in his work, asking her to help him prepare for an important educational conference.

Her response to an incident at the event is typical of Edith, with her high regard for personal freedom. The conference featured a debate between a psychologist named Wyneken, who was a rabid proponent of communal child rearing, and Stern, a proponent of family-based child rearing. The fanatical, melancholy Wyneken was bad enough, but his pupils, trotted out at the debate, had abandoned independent thought in favor of unquestioning obedience to their leader. This situation, more than anything, discredited Wyneken's theories in Edith's eyes.

The exhilarating summer of 1913 and the peaceful vacation in Breslau gave way to an unexpectedly difficult and solitary winter. The return to Göttingen proved more challenging than Edith had anticipated. Despair replaced confidence as she faced the enormous task she had set herself: To prepare for the state boards and to write the outline for her thesis.

The Dark Night of the Student

It wasn't exactly that Edith was in over her head. She had the intellectual resources to meet her goal. But when she added it all up—the memorization of material for the state boards, the independent thought necessary to complete her outline, the classes, and the loneliness imposed by the solitary nature of her work—the result was "a state of veritable despair."

She wasn't entirely on her own. She rented a room on the ground floor of a house a block from the home of her cousin Richard Courant and his wife, Nelli. If Richard noticed a light in her room when he walked by in the evening, he would tap on her window and stop for a visit. She kept up her contact with Mos and a few other friends. Reinach's lectures and his "Exercises for the Advanced" provided intellectual stimulation along with camaraderie.

The times spent in Reinach's classes were the happiest moments of Edith's days in Göttingen. Reinach lectured, but he also led open-ended discussions, drawing his students into a common search for the answers to particular philosophical questions. That semester, for example, they were considering the problem of motion. Reinach's status as a fellow seeker was so genuine that in the end, under the influence of his students, he abandoned his original position on this issue and started anew.

Once, when he asked Edith how she understood an aspect of the problem, she quietly gave her reply. He had arrived at the same conclusion and told her so in a friendly, encouraging way. "I could not have imagined a greater mark of distinction," Edith later reflected.

Husserl, who lacked Reinach's human touch, nevertheless was an effective if somewhat dull teacher. His course on Kant that semester was challenging enough to make Edith feel she was making substantial strides in her chosen field.

On the other hand, there was a distinct possibility she might crack under the strain. To her dismay, she discovered that she had forgotten much of the material she would need to have at her fingertips for the state boards. Not only did she have to get her Greek up to par; she also had to pursue a more wide-ranging review of history, German literature, and the history of philosophy than she had anticipated.

But it was her doctoral work that nearly undid her. For the first time she was face-to-face with a problem—the nature of empathy—that wouldn't give way to her determined efforts to understand and conquer it. She had boasted that her head was "harder than the thickest of walls," and now she was beating that head against a wall that refused to yield.

Books couldn't help her. The writings of Husserl and Lipps on the topic had nothing in common. She had to get a grip on the subject through her own intellectual effort before she could grasp the thinking of anyone else.

The struggle was so intense that sleep eluded her, a problem that was to plague her for years. The unceasing intellectual battle occupied days that ran from six in the morning to midnight and continued even during meals: Edith usually ate alone in order to reflect without interruption. She even kept a pen and paper on her nightstand for dream-induced brainstorms, but these notes never amounted to much in the cold light of day.

"All this brought me to a point where life itself seemed unbearable," she said. She welcomed the possibility of death. "I could no longer cross the street without wishing I would be run over by some vehicle. And when we went on an excursion, I hoped I would fall off a cliff and not return alive."

Husserl was no help. Edith reported on her progress several times over the semester, but the Master invariably went off on a tangent after Edith said only a few words. By the time he had talked himself out, he was too tired to listen to her. (William Bell, a friend also working under Husserl, told Edith his method for handling these discussions: When Bell had to report on his dissertation, he would get Husserl to go out for a walk. The older man would become so winded as they climbed the hills that Bell could speak without interruption.)

In the end, it was Reinach who saved the day. On the advice of Mos—who knew Edith was dissatisfied with her work but not that she was tormented—Edith asked Reinach whether she could discuss her situation with him. He readily agreed. Shortly after, when the down-hearted Edith laid out her research and reflections, Reinach couldn't have been more encouraging. In fact, he urged her to start writing and to return to him at the end of the semester, only three weeks away, to update him on her progress.

Edith, though still depressed, did so. She went back at the appointed time, only to find her mentor made her sit and wait while he read the manuscript. Then the impossible happened: "Very good, Fräulein Stein," he said.

Edith was shocked. Reinach liked it so much that he urged her to stay at Göttingen over the upcoming vacation until she finished it. He himself would look at it when he returned home from a visit to his parents.

With her confidence restored, Edith finished the draft in a week. An early-evening rain had begun to fall when she put down her pen at last. Relieved, but with her nerves strained to the limit, she decided to go to Reinach's house to ask his wife when he was scheduled to return.

Just as she rounded the corner, a taxi pulled up the street. In the distance she saw Reinach get out and go into his house. "That told me enough; I swung around and went home. It is impossible to express how much joy and gratitude I felt; even today, more than twenty years later, I can still draw some of that deep sigh of relief."

When Edith showed up with the thesis the next morning, Reinach read it and enthusiastically approved it. She could use it as one of the two theses she would need for her state boards, he told her. Better, Husserl himself would be impressed with the work, for he rarely got papers of such high caliber.

Edith felt "like one reborn." "Nothing I had accomplished so far," she wrote, "had ever exacted such a heavy toll in mental effort." Only those who engaged in similar creative philosophical work could appreciate the demands it made, she said.

Reassured by Reinach's endorsement, Edith was able to shift her attention from the manuscript to preparation for the oral exams. First, however, she took a well-earned vacation in Breslau.

Twilight of Peace

Yet vacations are not always everything the vacationer hopes for. It was during this trip home that the Steins' brother-in-law, Max, demanded that the family come and take Else back. Not only did Edith then have to endure the difficult retrieval of her sister from Hamburg; she had to live with the stress of Else's presence in the house on Michaelisstrasse. Everyone was tense, too, wondering if the couple would be able to resolve their differences. Edith, as focused as ever, managed to put these concerns aside so that she could study for the state boards while at home.

She also formed a new friendship there that brought out her compassion and friendliness, traits that many found so attractive in Edith. Toni Meyer was an intelligent woman, more than a decade older than Edith, and a student of psychology and philosophy. She lived in Breslau with her mother, a wealthy widow, and studied under Stern.

Toni was mentally ill. She didn't disclose this to Edith initially, but Edith already knew by way of the grapevine (a business friend had told Auguste). Edith noted the fatigue that occasionally transfigured Toni's face, the drooping eyelids, and the heavy way she walked, "as though her feet were tied together."

When Edith first met her, though, Toni's condition was stable, the illness nearly imperceptible. Toni was headed to Göttingen to study phenomenology, and when Edith returned to her room of the previous semester, Toni rented an elegant flat nearby. They ate their meals together at a private dining room and took walks. Toni, eager to support the overworked Edith, regularly supplied fresh flowers for Edith's room. In all, Edith said, her friend's concern made the semester a "sunny" one for her.

After a few weeks back in Göttingen, Toni, in the interest of honesty, revealed her condition. She would understand if Edith wanted to break off the friendship. "I told Toni that this fact could in no way frighten me away," Edith later recalled. "My reassurance obviously lightened her heart. Now at last she could enjoy our friendship without reservation. It seemed to her ... a great boon that a young, healthy, and well-endowed person should treat her as an equal."

Edith's affection for her friend was unfeigned. In her quiet, direct way, she appreciated Toni for herself, illness and all. A few years later, when the older woman's condition deteriorated, doctors diagnosed her as manic-depressive. Edith visited her when she was confined to various mental institutions. She persevered through Toni's bouts of paranoia, valiantly trying to discern how much of the patient's imaginative conversation about her medical care was fact and how much fiction.

Toni's companionship enlivened the summer semester of 1914, but it helped that Edith had already emerged from the gloom that shrouded her preliminary doctoral work. She actually enjoyed studying for the boards, meeting with friends so they could quiz one another as they walked the hills of Göttingen. These friends also taught her how to cram for tests, something the brainy Edith had apparently never had to do before. With almost childlike wonder, she discovered the technique of underlining—red for the important material, red and blue for the intermediate information, and red, blue, and green for the most critical. She could isolate "an unbelievable amount" of material this way, she said with delight.

Edith's academic and social life had been back on track for only a few months when this innocent world came to an unexpected and sudden end. On June 28, Serbian terrorists assassinated the Archduke Francis Ferdinand, heir to the Austro-Hungarian throne, and his wife while they were visiting Sarajevo. "Our placid student life was blown to bits by the Serbian assassination of royalty," Edith would later write. "July was dominated by the question: Will war break out in Europe?" Few realized that for all practical purposes, World War I was already underway.

Given the growing nationalism, militarism, divisive alliances, treaties, and ententes dominating Europe for the previous decades, war was inevitable. But the students found this hard to believe. "No one growing up during or since the war can possibly imagine the security in which we assumed ourselves to be living before 1914," Edith wrote. The world was stable, comfortable, built on peace, and sustained by such basic rights as the ownership of property.

If war did come, Edith concluded, it would be different from previous wars: New weapons and machinery would make the fighting extremely destructive. "It would all be over in a few months," she said, a common expectation in those days that would make the four years of butchery still ahead even harder to bear.

Edith was a staunch patriot, as were all her friends. Reinach was among the first to enlist, telling a friend who asked him whether he must go, "It's not that I *must;* rather, I'm permitted to go." Edith, who was present, was pleased with this sentiment, since it echoed her own feelings.

The days following the assassinations were tense and uncertain, but Edith handled them with typical fortitude. "I had already formed a habit then, which later I practiced quite consciously in such times of crisis; calmly, I went about my ordinary duties, but deep inside I was prepared to call a halt to them at any moment. It went against the grain for me to increase the common agitation by running around or by useless chatter."[1]

On July 30, she was sitting at her desk reading Schopenhauer's *The World as Will and Idea* when word came that war had been declared. That same night, Edith was on a train bound for Breslau, motivated more by patriotism than concerns for family or safety. She reasoned that Göttingen, located in central Germany, would probably sleep through the war. Breslau, near the Russian border, was likely to be under attack any day. She wanted to be where the action was.

"I have no private life anymore," she told herself. "All my energy must be devoted to this great happening. Only when the war is over, if I'm alive then, will I be permitted to think of my private affairs once more." [2]

And with that romantic but sincere statement, Edith put her life on hold. Her zigzag academic career had taken yet another unexpected turn.

SEVEN

EDITH GOES TO WAR

As soon as Edith was back in Breslau, she signed up for a nurse's aide course tailored to meet the needs of the war effort. The four-week session covered communicable diseases, surgery, bandaging, and the art of giving injections, but only in a cursory manner, given the limited time. Edith supplemented the material with Erna's atlas of anatomy and other medical textbooks. Then she visited Erna at the hospital to receive additional practice in bandaging.

She volunteered at the local hospital in the tuberculosis and surgery wards and also in a ward devoted mostly to children who had been "run over," presumably by the still relatively new phenomenon, the automobile. Edith "got the impression that the sick were not used to getting loving attention" and filled in the gap any way she could.

Meanwhile, Edith told the Red Cross that she was totally at their disposal. "All I wanted," she said, "was to go as soon and as far away as possible, preferably to a field hospital at the front." But there were too many volunteers at that point and too few victims of war. The wholesale slaughter that marked World War I was yet to come.

In the course of her volunteer work, she soon caught one of the diseases she had been studying—bronchitis—making her ineligible for immediate service. When she finally recovered, the Red Cross still didn't need her, and the winter semester at Göttingen was nearly underway. So two months after consecrating herself to the war effort, Edith was back at the university. "My attitude had in no way changed," she said of this turn of events. "I would have welcomed a call away from my books any day."

But with no hope of that in sight, she decided that she might as well get the state boards out of the way. The exams seemed "ridiculously trivial compared to the current events which kept us on tenterhooks," she said. Trivial or not, they beat the tedium of hanging around Breslau, waiting for a call to arms.

Many of her friends at Göttingen had received that call, however, and were away at the front. Her cousin, Richard Courant, was among the first to ship out, and his wife, Nelli, had returned to Breslau to be with her widowed father. The young couple insisted that Edith use their attractive apartment in Göttingen.

This was bounty beyond the usual meager student lodgings, and Edith gladly accepted. Nelli told her to enjoy the place and to help herself to their well-stocked cupboards. Edith did so. When she entertained, she took care to set a beautiful table, raiding Nellie's stock of linens, silver trays, vases, fruit baskets, and anything else that would help set a pleasant mood in the dark times.

In spite of the national circumstances, there were still opportunities to entertain. Edith had met Pauline Reinach, Adolf Reinach's sister, during a previous semester, and the two were now friends. Pauline was "lively, witty, and quick" in social settings, but in their private conversations, Edith discovered "a deep, quiet, and truly contemplative soul." (This proved truer than Edith could have anticipated. Pauline later converted from Judaism to Catholicism and became a Benedictine nun.)

Pauline was back at Göttingen to study, as was Erika Gothe, whom Edith knew from the Philosophical Society. (She said that

Erika's attitude of thoughtful silence in that group appealed to her very much.) The three joined forces and shared meals together at Pauline's boarding house. "The friendship with Pauline and Erika had more depth and beauty than my former student friendships," Edith said. "For the first time, I was not the one to lead or to be sought after; but rather I saw in others something better and higher than myself."

The women not only studied and socialized together, they also prepared packages for their friends in the military. At Christmas, they collected breads, cakes, and delicacies from Göttingen's bakeries and wrapped them in colorful paper tied with silk ribbons. These packages, according to shipping regulations, had to be sewn in burlap for delivery. "We were stretched out on the floor in Pauline's room," she later recalled, "until past midnight, to accomplish this requirement in the most expert fashion."

When Edith met with another friend to study for the boards, the two of them knitted socks and other items for the soldiers while they analyzed the Punic Wars or discussed the impact on history of the Greek city-state. The men in turn kept up a steady correspondence with their supporters. Once, Reinach folded into his letter delicate flowers known as snowdrops for each of the women in Pauline's circle. "He had picked them himself, and they were still fresh when they arrived."

Days of Reckoning

Edith turned in her theses for the boards in November and scheduled the oral exams for the first available dates, January 14 and 15. The tests would last at least an hour each and would be conducted by professors in her specialties: philosophy, history, and German literature. There was another required set of exams in "general culture," which covered philosophy, German literature, and religion. She was exempt from these since she would already be examined in the first two, and Jews were not examined in the last, religion. "Therefore," she commented dryly, "I was spared having to prove I had 'general culture.'"

When the days for the tests arrived, Edith was a bundle of nerves. She confided this to her cleaning lady, "who plunked all her ponderous self down on the chaise lounge and gave me a pep talk." Encouraged, Edith was off to prove her competence in the field of German literature. She needn't have worried. She read and translated the archaic German of an earlier age fluently and described the rest of the test as "a stroll through German literature."

The next day proved more challenging. During the philosophy exam, Husserl threw her a curve. Because Chairman Miller, head of the examining committee and a formidable man, would be acting as proctor for this session, Husserl feared Miller might accuse him of being too easygoing in examining his own student. Husserl therefore grilled Edith relentlessly.

As luck would have it, he quizzed her at length on Plato's *Timeaus*, which she had never read but only heard about in lectures, rather than on one of the many selections of Plato that she had read. She didn't want to embarrass Husserl by admitting to this. "I began rather boldly to construct the thought process of the dialogue by using the questions he put to me as my point of departure."

Undaunted, she did the same when Husserl asked her about some works of David Hume, one of which she was not too familiar with. "I enjoyed these feats of mental acrobatics," she said, "but they demanded tremendous effort."

Exhausted by the session, she nevertheless had one more exam to go. When she showed up for her history test, the proctor—Richard Weissenfels, one of her teachers—had not yet arrived. The examiner started without him, testing Edith on her knowledge of Greek history.

When Weissenfels turned up, the examiner told him that "the lady is well informed in Greek." "The lady is well-informed in general," Weissenfels remarked with a laugh. In that spirit, the quizzing continued, and Edith easily acquitted herself.

Pauline Reinach, who waited outside the examining room, took her to a coffeehouse, the *Kron und Lanz*, "to revive me after winning the battle." In fact, Edith had passed *summa cum laude*. That night, on the way to a celebratory dinner with her friends, Edith stopped to send her mother a telegram with the news.

Auguste quickly wrote back to congratulate her. She suggested to Edith that she give some thought to "the One," God, who stood behind her success. "For me," Edith said, "it had not come to that yet."

Besides, the question of "the One," at this point, took a back seat to a more immediate circumstance: The Red Cross needed her at last. Would she be willing to serve in Austria at a hospital for soldiers who had contracted infectious diseases?

A Taste of War

Edith accepted the offer without hesitation. Her mother protested. When Edith ignored her mother's pleas, Auguste advanced her most powerful argument: lice. The soldiers would be crawling with them, and Edith would soon be crawling with them as well. As a matter of fact, Edith dreaded this possibility, but it didn't stop her.

Finally, Auguste said: "You will not go with my permission."

Edith stoutly replied: "Then I must go without your permission."

"Granite was striking granite," Edith later said of that moment. Auguste knew she had been defeated and moped around for a few days. However, soon she was helping her daughter pull together the supplies she would need.

Frieda purchased fabric and patterns and sewed nurse's uniforms for her sister. Erna vaccinated Edith against typhoid and cholera. On April 7, she was off for Mahrisch-Weisskirchen, the site of the hospital, a six-hour train ride from Breslau.

The hospital was located in a former riding academy for the cavalry and at the time of Edith's arrival served primarily as an isolation unit. The hundreds of soldiers shipped here suffered from such highly contagious and virulent diseases as typhoid, cholera, and dysentery. In previous wars, these illnesses had often killed more soldiers than those who died in combat. Vaccinations would largely eliminate that threat, but in Austria the vaccination program had not caught up with the recruits. When it did, fewer men succumbed, and the hospital would change its focus to care for the wounded.

For her first three months, however, Edith worked on the typhoid ward. The disease is usually transmitted through bodily waste. This presented a problem, since the aides couldn't avoid such contact in the course of caring for their patients. But Edith had great confidence in disinfectants and the simple expedient of washing her hands after touching one patient and before touching another. "Infection," she said flatly, "is a sign of lack of cleanliness."

She was more concerned with a different threat: that posed by the romantic entanglements among a number of the doctors, nurses, aides, and maids who staffed the hospital. Edith had only been at

Mahrisch-Weisskirchen a few days before she had her first taste of life in the off-hours. Some of the workers were throwing a farewell party for a doctor and invited Edith. She didn't want to go, but her superior urged her to, saying that a refusal of her first invitation might provoke resentment.

Edith showed up and immediately had misgivings. A large table held fruit, tortes, and an abundance of liquor bottles. Edith, who never drank alcohol, stuck with cake and fruit and watched as the evening deteriorated. "One doctor held one of the nurses, who wanted no more to drink, by the head and poured liquor into her. I became more and more uneasy. What all might follow?"

Edith and the guest of honor, a young Polish doctor, were the only two sober members of the group. "What must you think of me?" he asked, embarrassed. Finally, he walked her back to her dorm and safety. After this, Edith concentrated on work and left the socializing to others.

She was good at the work. Recovery from typhoid rested on excellent nursing care because, at that time, there was little relief available from medicine. Edith spoon-fed some patients, giving egg mixed with cognac to the most seriously ill. In patients whose typhoid progressed into pneumonia or pleurisy, the heart often threatened to quit, so in those cases she gave injections of camphor, sometimes hourly.

Edith changed sheets, bathed those who were completely helpless, shifted barely conscious men from one bed to another by herself ("this could be done rather easily if one went about it correctly"), and tended the most critical cases "as one would little children." When the mouth of one especially sick soldier repeatedly filled with bloody mucus, Edith carefully wiped it out whenever she was near his bed. "A look from him always expressed his gratitude for this small service of love."

She had to be ready for anything. Once, when she worked the night shift, a delirious patient kept struggling to his feet to run away. "I had no alternative but to tie him up. I stretched a sheet tightly across the bed and tied the four corners to the bedposts. Only the restless patient's head now showed."

If a patient died, as sometimes happened when Edith was on duty, she handled her responsibilities by the book, calling for a doctor to certify the death, arranging for the removal of the body, and getting rid of the bed linen. The death of one patient, however, gave her pause. The husky soldier had not been conscious since his admission to the hospital. When he died, Edith gathered his things together.

"A small piece of paper slipped out of the man's notebook and fell in front of me," she wrote. "His wife had given it to him to take along; on it was a prayer for the preservation of his life. Only when I saw that did I fully realize what this death meant, humanly speaking. But I dared not let myself brood over that."

The doctors liked her. A Dr. Pick, in particular, rewarded her intelligent curiosity by giving her bedside lectures as if she were a medical student. "One discovery he enjoyed very much was that he could talk Latin to me as he might have to a colleague. Naturally it was the barbaric kind of Latin produced when the medical men murdered the language."

Later, when Edith was assigned to the surgical ward, the doctors there were just as appreciative. One day, a transport of wounded soldiers arrived. All hands were on deck—including many doctors not accustomed to operating—and Edith worked into the night, assisting them. She had picked up basic operating techniques from observation. "One young woman doctor who was totally green at surgery stationed herself very close to me so I could give her the necessary directions."

After nearly six months at the hospital, Edith was exhausted. More troubling than that, however, was the nagging thought that perhaps it was time to return to her academic work. Admissions to the hospital had dropped as the fighting shifted elsewhere. There were more than enough aides available to do the kind of work she was doing.

Did the war effort really need her? If it didn't, wouldn't it be better to "do that for which one has the requisite talents"? This was the dictum she had laid down not many years before when puzzling over a career path.

The problem resolved itself in an unexpected manner. Edith took what was intended to be a furlough, returning to Breslau to be with her family. The staff at Weisskirchen agreed to recall her when they needed her.

At home, not wanting to waste time actually resting, she began to brush up on her Greek. She had to pass an exam in the language in order to continue in her doctoral work. Edith got the test out of the way a few weeks later and passed easily.

Still, she had not heard from Weisskirchen. Shortly after, she learned that the hospital had closed because of a decrease in military action in the area. Although Edith applied to the Red Cross for another placement, she was never called up.

The decision was now out of her hands. She would devote herself to her doctoral thesis, but decided to work on it in Breslau instead of returning to Göttingen: "I would be ready to comply immediately were I to be called for service again."

EIGHT

BACK ON TRACK

Nearly two years had passed since that depressing winter of 1913–14, when Edith had struggled to come to grips with the notion of empathy. Now, late in 1915, the world was an even darker place. Friends had died in battle—among them an art instructor from Göttingen, two members of the Philosophical Society, and, early in 1916, Husserl's seventeen-year-old son, Wolfgang.

The teenager had volunteered for the army and died at Flanders. His mother once told Edith that she had never worried about Wolfgang because she knew that "wherever he might be or whatever his occupation, he would make those around him happy." Husserl was devastated. "One has to bear up," he said.

Reinach, away at the front, was no longer on hand to dispel the gloom with encouraging insights. Mos, chief resident at a hospital for the mentally ill, found wartime stress and the burden of his responsibilities too much. He suffered a nervous breakdown and gradually withdrew from Edith.

Then came the stunning news that Nelli Courant had filed for divorce from Edith's cousin, Richard. Nelli's essentially petty reasons included her assertion that Richard was not serious about his career as a mathematician. (During the Nazi era, Richard emigrated to New York for a job teaching at New York University. He developed a strong graduate program in mathematics at NYU, and the Courant Institute for Math and Computer Sciences there is named for him.) Now, in the throes of divorce, both Courants turned to Edith for sympathy.

She had the consolation of living with her family on Michaelisstrasse, but even so these painful realities cut her, she said, "to the quick." Resolutely, she pushed all distractions aside and turned to her doctoral dissertation. The specter of her earlier effort haunted her. Would depression and confusion dog her again?

To her relief, once she started to work, everything fell into place. Recalling that time, she later wrote:

Oh, what a difference compared to my former efforts! Of course, each morning I seated myself at my desk with some trepidation. I was like a tiny dot in limitless space. Would anything come to me out of this great expanse—anything which I could grasp? I lay as far back as I could in my chair and strenuously focused my mind on what at the moment I deemed the most vital question. After awhile it seemed as though light began to dawn. Then, I was able, at least, to formulate a question and to find ways to attack it.

Soon, not only was she composing, she was enjoying it. "The writing would bring a rosy glow to my face, and an unfamiliar feeling of happiness surged through me.... Every day I felt that the ability to continue my work was like a new gift."[1]

She kept at it for three months, into January 1916. And then one day she felt that "something had detached itself from me and formed an existence on its own." Her dissertation had come to life. It needed refinement, but she was nearly ready to present it to Husserl and to schedule the round of exams required for a doctorate.

Before she could do so, unexpected news arrived: Husserl had accepted a call to take the philosophy chair at the University of Freiburg-im-Breisgau. He would be leaving Göttingen immediately for the prestigious post, one of the most important philosophy positions in Germany.

Another Fork in the Road

The announcement "canceled out all my plans at one stroke," Edith said. She had assumed that she would be getting her doctorate at Göttingen. She wanted to stick to that plan rather than deal with a new set of circumstances and new, unfamiliar examiners.

She wrote to Husserl asking that he allow her to come to Göttingen immediately so that she could qualify for her doctorate there. He wrote back. What's the hurry? he asked. The faculty at Freiburg—who would conduct her exams—would treat his doctoral candidates kindly, he assured her. She would have to come to Freiburg and qualify there, not at Göttingen.

This was a blow, but a bigger one followed. Her old high school needed her as a substitute teacher for the upper-level Latin classes. The war had thinned the ranks of teachers, and even though Edith wasn't certified, her reputation for academic excellence lingered.

The principal, one of her former instructors, pleaded with her: "O my dear Fräulein," he said, hand over his heart. "You have always been capable of anything; you will know how to do this also."

The idea of abandoning full-time work on her dissertation dismayed Edith. On the other hand, in its way, this was an opportunity to contribute to the war effort. In early February, she took on a full load of classes "totally unhampered by any prior training in pedagogy."

Edith was a success, as the principal had predicted. She was enthusiastic and knew the material in depth. She demanded excellence.

Some of the students had a poor grasp of Latin due to a rapid changeover of teachers the previous year. When most of these failed a translation test, they clamored for a make-up exam, a right guaranteed them according to a new education ministry regulation. "Oh no," Edith said, insisting they actually learn the material, not simply have another go at a test. She ignored the regulation.

The girls liked her. Edith had been a student in the same school only five years before and easily sympathized with the concerns of teenagers. She was also savvy enough to dress well. "After all," she said, "I stood at the desk in front of grown girls" all day. "I knew how closely they scrutinized one's appearance."

If Edith was ambivalent about her new career, Auguste was not. At last, her daughter's uncertain journey—from dropout to psychology major to philosophy major to Red Cross aide to dissertation writer—had come to a satisfying, possibly permanent, conclusion. Or so Auguste hoped. Now Edith could settle in Breslau, back in her old circle of friends, in her old school, and in a profession the family actually understood, unlike her philosophical work.

But Edith was beginning to sink under the heavy workload. When she got home each day from teaching, she struggled with her dissertation until dinner. After that, she returned to the dissertation until ten, when she turned her attention to classes for the next day. Auguste unsuccessfully tried to send her to bed at a reasonable hour each night.

As the strain grew, Edith came to a conclusion: "In the long run, a combination of teaching with simultaneous, serious research was impossible." If she could produce a worthy dissertation, she would give up teaching for the life of a scholar.

A Clear Path at Last … Maybe

Edith put the finishing touches on her dissertation by Easter and dictated it to two of her cousins. They typed it up and mailed it off to Husserl. If he would read it by the summer, she proposed, she would come at that time to take the oral exams.

She left for Freiburg almost immediately after school closed at the beginning of July. "I cannot express how deep was my relief as I put the school behind me. I discovered that vacation time is far, far more enjoyable for the teacher than for the children."

She visited friends on the way, briefly meeting up with Hans Lipps from the Philosophical Society, who was on furlough from the army. Although it seemed that Edith still secretly loved Hans, their meeting brought religious rather than romantic issues to the fore.

Back when they were students in Göttingen, Edith had "learned to respect questions of faith and persons who had faith." She even occasionally went to Protestant churches with friends, although the political nature of the sermons turned her off. "I had not yet found a way back to God," Edith wrote of that period, but Lipps must have sensed her spiritual questioning.

They had arranged to meet for a friendly chat at the train station in Dresden. As they caught up on old friends, he asked if she were part of that circle of their former colleagues who went to Mass every day. He meant philosophers such as Dietrich von Hildebrand, who were converts "now proving to be very zealous."

No, she "was not one of them," she told Hans. "Very nearly I added, 'Unfortunately.'" And she said no more about it. Whatever religious inclination she might have had, she quietly tucked her feelings under the mantle of her intellect and proceeded on to Freiburg.

Freiburg, close to the French border, is a long journey by train from Breslau. Apart from the visit with Lipps, Edith nearly regretted making the trip. As it turned out, not only had Husserl failed to read her thesis; he didn't have time to think about her exams. He was new to the university, after all, and he had not quite settled in.

"She can get her doctorate next time," he told his wife, who protested her husband's cavalier treatment of his star pupil. Meanwhile, he suggested that Edith stay in Freiburg a bit and take his course on modern philosophy. Edith, feeling that a break would come her way, remained calm and did stay for the course.

Within a short time, Frau Husserl had won the day. "My wife gives me no peace!" the Master told Edith one day. "I am to take the time to read your work."

And he did, declaring it was much more than just a student's paper, as Edith had modestly described it. "No, definitely not just that," he said. "I find you to be very independent." That gave Edith hope. If Husserl approved her dissertation, she only needed to pass the oral exams, scheduled for early August.

Before that outcome could unfold, however, the path of Edith's life took yet another turn. A friend told her that Husserl needed an assistant, someone to organize the thousands of papers that lay heaped around his house. These philosophical essays and scraps of thought were written in shorthand and were practically indecipherable to Husserl, whose eyesight had grown weak. Ordinarily, at the time, this would have been a man's job, but all the men were away at war. Edith decided to put herself forward for the position.

One day, she happened to be walking through town with Husserl. He told her not only that her thesis was excellent and she herself very gifted, but also that her thinking anticipated some of his own as-yet-unpublished work. She decided the moment had come. She offered her services.

They were just crossing the Dreisam River, and the Master came to a standstill in the middle of the bridge. "You want to help me?" he said, delighted. "Yes! With you I would enjoy working!"

"I do not know which one of us was more elated," Edith later said. "We were like a young couple at the moment of their betrothal."

The doctoral process took a backseat to this exciting development, and Edith passed the oral exams easily. On August 3, 1916, she received her doctorate *summa cum laude* from the University of Freiburg. Husserl was "beaming with joy" at a celebratory party that night, and Frau Husserl placed on Edith's head a victor's wreath of ivy and daisies.

Soon, in a manner of speaking, the party would continue. Edith would wrap up her teaching in Breslau and return to Freiburg by October, assistant to the man she considered "one of those real giants who transcend their own time and who determine history."

In the long run, it would turn out that the history he would determine would in some measure be her own. And it wouldn't be to her immediate liking.

NINE

THE TRUTH AT LAST

Word of Edith's triumph spread quickly among her friends. Within two weeks, Fritz Kaufmann congratulated her in a letter from the front. She wrote back immediately to thank him. She was troubled, she said, that life should be "heaping" such good fortune on her while others suffered the trials of war.

On the other hand, she was particularly pleased at the opportunity to work with Husserl. "Obviously, he has no clear idea as yet how we will actually work together," she wrote. Had she but known, she might have added, "and that lack is what will eventually doom this project." But she didn't know, and her enthusiasm carried her along for a few months.

The autobiography Edith would later write, *Life in a Jewish Family*, ends abruptly as she leaves Freiburg for Breslau on the day after receiving her doctorate. She had started writing the book shortly before entering the convent in 1933, but the demands of convent life and the outbreak of World War II kept her from finishing the work. Fortunately, she was an inveterate letter writer, and much of her story emerges through her correspondence.

The philosopher Roman Ingarden, her friend since the Göttingen days, stayed in close touch. As early as January 1917, on the job only three months, Edith told him by letter of "the dear Master's sudden and variable fancies." Plainly put, these amounted to his refusal to review systematically the material Edith so carefully pulled together and placed before him. The demands of teaching and the rigors of philosophizing—rather than any absence of goodwill on his part—prevented him from entering into a collaborative process with Edith.

Collaboration was what Husserl had agreed to. Edith wasn't in Freiburg as a secretary, even though she was intent on organizing Husserl's papers. But the papers were for the most part in unpublishable form, some just bits of paper dating to 1903. The material needed serious attention from Husserl and give-and-take between master and disciple. Only someone like Edith, deeply schooled in phenomenological thought, could provide the sort of discussion, writing, and editing the task demanded.

"Collaboration with the dear Master is a highly complicated matter," she wrote to Fritz Kaufmann. "There is a concern that it will never come to an actual *collaboration*. He keeps occupying himself with individual questions about which he dutifully informs me, but he cannot be moved, even once, to look at the draft I am making for him out of his old material."[1]

She decided to plunge ahead "with or without him" in order to get the papers into an accessible form. In the course of Edith's nearly one and a half years with Husserl, she did manage to prepare two of his manuscripts for publication. She also began teaching classes on the fundamentals of phenomenology to students interested in joining Husserl's seminars.

"I am to become here—this was expressed to me with touching naïvete—what Reinach was in Göttingen," Edith wrote to Ingarden. Of course, there was only one Reinach, but Edith recognized the important and similar role she played in mediating between Husserl and his young students.

Another very practical obstacle would get in the way of Edith's becoming what Reinach had been. As a woman, she could not get appointed to a professorship at the university level. Women had only recently been allowed into university studies; it would be some years before the barriers to faculty appointment fell.

Nevertheless, Edith began pursuing this possibility immediately. Over the course of several years, she approached the universities at Göttingen, Freiburg, and Breslau. Even a recommendation from Husserl failed to make a difference.

This was too bad, because the arrangement in Freiburg proved inevitably to be unworkable. The final straw came in February 1918. The Master seemed to view her work as primarily organizational, she told Ingarden.

One day, he "favored" her with detailed instructions—"in a most friendly manner, but I simply cannot bear that kind of thing"—on how to proceed. She balked. "Basically," she said to Ingarden, "it is the thought of being at someone's disposition that I cannot bear."

I can place myself at the service of something, and I can do all manner of things for the love of someone, but to be at the service of a person—in short, to obey—is something I cannot do. And if Husserl will not accustom himself once more to treat me as a collaborator in the work—as I have always considered our situation to be and he, in theory, did likewise—then we shall have to part company.[2]

They did indeed part company, but without rancor. Edith never lost her affection for Husserl, nor he for her. "For me, he will always remain the Master, whose image cannot be blurred by any human weakness," she wrote to Fritz Kaufmann.

A Glimmer of Light

Shortly before Edith made her decision to leave Husserl, devastating news arrived from Flanders: Adolf Reinach had been killed in battle. He and his wife, Anna, had become Christians a few years before, and Reinach's interests had shifted from philosophy to theology. He had looked forward, after the war, to pursuing religious studies. As it was, he'd left numerous philosophical papers behind, and Anna wanted Edith to come to Göttingen to put these in order.

In the spring of 1918 she did so, even though she dreaded the trip because she was sure she would find Anna broken and distraught. Instead, she found the widow grieving but unshaken. "It was then that I first encountered the cross and the divine strength it inspires in those who bear it," Edith later said. "For the first time I saw before my very eyes the Church, born of Christ's redemptive suffering, victorious over the sting of death. It was the moment in which my unbelief was shattered.... Christ streamed out upon me: Christ in the mystery of the cross." [3]

But even though her unbelief was shattered, Edith could not come to grips with what that meant for her life. Over the next two years, she groped her way painfully toward full faith.

Prior to Reinach's death, she had been investigating the possibility of religious belief. She read both the Old and New Testaments and considered returning to Judaism. That option didn't satisfy her, although she had only to look at her mother's rock-like faith, sustained in spite of enormous hardship, to see the depth available to her there.

An incident that took place around this time influenced her much the way her encounter with Anna Reinach had done, although not so dramatically. Edith was visiting Frankfurt with Pauline Reinach, and the two stopped to see the Catholic cathedral there. A woman came in carrying bundles from shopping and knelt to pray for a few minutes. As unexceptional as this was, Edith had never seen anything like it. There was something unforgettable about this woman's interrupting her day to stop in at church as if for an "intimate conversation."

Perhaps, even then, Edith longed for the quiet simplicity of that unknown woman's faith. But her intellect demanded satisfaction, so she continued to mine philosophy for every possible truth regarding the state of humanity and the existence of God. The search was exhausting on an intellectual level—Edith never did anything by half measures. It was also exacerbated by the national and international situation as World War I ground on.

Roman Ingarden remembered Edith as a thoroughgoing patriot who "went through the entire war with the attitude of someone always on the verge of beginning a one-man battle." Edith was so eager to serve the war effort that during the time she worked in Freiburg she sent him "letter after letter asking whether she had the right to waste her time on philosophy and other such nonsense when there were people out there dying whom she should be helping." [4]

By mid-1918, with Germany's defeat increasingly imminent, a spirit of depression hovered over the country. A family friend committed suicide (the suicide rate rose substantially during the last days of the war), and Edith wrote to her sister Erna in the wake of their friend's death. She urged her to put aside pessimism.

✗ 3   "I want to affirm the value of life more than ever," she wrote in indirect testimony to her own ongoing transformation. Since wartime is uncertain, she told Erna, people have to accept that they might not survive to the end. "But that's no excuse to despair, either. If only we didn't limit our vision to the little bit of life in front of us, and then, only to what's immediately visible on the surface."[5]

Her family noticed her growing optimism as well as her solicitude for others—apparent, for example, in her willingness to set aside her own work to help Anna Reinach. They even referred to her as "saintly," although they assumed she was still without faith. "You have too high an opinion of me," she wrote to Erna. "I am not at all a saint and have my hours of weakness, just as everyone else does."

Along with those hours of weakness, however, she now had the impressive beginnings of a religious outlook. She told Erna that people shouldn't be upset if things go contrary to their expectations. "When that happens, one ought to think of what one still has, and also, that one is only here on a visit, as it were, that everything that depresses one so terribly now will not be all that important at the end; or it will have a totally different meaning [from what] we now recognize."[6]

In spite of these brave words, Edith continued to vacillate. Nothing seemed to be going right, and even if it wasn't "all that important in the end," she still had to get through the present. Her investigation of faith continued not only against a background of war and military defeat but also against a certain level of professional failure.

After the University of Göttingen rejected her application for a teaching position, she wrote to Kaufmann: "I am not *crushed*. I only regret that I am again faced with a decision about what to do in the future." Ultimately she wound up back in Breslau tutoring, lecturing, and giving private classes in philosophy. This she did, she said, "for want of anything better."

She also wrote scholarly articles—including "Psychic Causality" and "The Individual and the Community"—that reveal her intense commitment to phenomenology as well as her interior struggles. For example, she wrote in "Psychic Causality": "There is a state of resting in God, an absolute break from all intellectual activity, when one forms no plans ... when one simply hands over the future to God's will and 'surrenders himself to fate.' I myself have experienced this state to some extent."[7]

#4a

The Final Crisis

Edith wrote "Psychic Causality" in 1919, as one of the requirements for applying to Göttingen for a teaching position. Throughout all of 1920, she was in the final stages of the struggle she described there: to "hand over the future to God's will." Only this time, she was to hand it over, not "to some extent," but entirely.

She spent that year in Breslau as the whole family pitched in to prepare for Erna and Hans' wedding, scheduled for early December. "To be sure, I was on tenterhooks the whole time," Edith wrote in *Life in a Jewish Family*. "I was passing through a personal crisis which was totally concealed from my relatives.... My health was very poor, probably as a result of the spiritual conflicts I then endured in complete secrecy and without any human support."

The wedding took place at home in Edith's study, converted into a "marriage hall." The print hanging on the wall above where the bride sat happened to be Cimabue's painting of St. Francis. Arno had suggested removing it prior to the wedding—probably feeling that "the saint was not exactly an appropriate witness for a Jewish wedding," Edith observed—but she told him to leave it. "I looked at St. Francis [during the ceremony] and found great consolation in his presence," she said.

Now that her beloved sister was married, Edith decided the time had come to take care of herself. She arranged to spend the following summer with Hedwig Conrad-Martius and her husband at their farm in Bergzabern. These old friends from the Göttingen days owned a fruit farm and relied on their friends to help with the harvest. A steady stream of philosophers came through the place each season to pick apples during the day and philosophize at night. Edith was a frequent guest.

The Conrad-Martius family was now Lutheran, having converted to Christianity some years before. They were quietly supportive of their friend's religious journey. One day they left for a brief trip and suggested that she curl up with a book from their library.

Edith went to the bookcase. "I picked at random and took out a large volume. It bore the title *The Life of St. Teresa of Avila, Written by Herself.* I began to read, was at once captivated, and did not stop until I reached the end. As I closed the book, I said, 'That is the truth.'"[8]

That same day, she bought a missal and a Catholic catechism, studied both, and soon after attended her first Mass. "Thanks to my previous study, I understood even the smallest ceremonies," she said. After Mass she followed the priest out and "asked him without more ado for baptism."

He inquired about the extent of her instruction. "The only reply I could make was, 'Please ... test my knowledge.'" He did and was astonished by her understanding. They set the date of baptism for January 1, 1922. This would allow time for her formal preparation.

The delay did not disturb Edith. On the contrary, it gave her time to consider the terrible issue now before her: how to break the news to her mother.

TEN

Nearly a Nun, But Not Quite

People who become saints after undergoing conversion sometimes write about the experience, giving insight into what triggered their decision. Venerable Charles de Foucauld, for example, the founder of the Little Brothers of Jesus, abandoned a dissolute life to return to the faith. "The moment I realized God existed," he said, "I knew I could not do otherwise than live for him alone."

St. Augustine, the fifth-century bishop and theologian, described his dramatic conversion in chapter eight of his *Confessions*. He wrote at length of his struggle to be freed from "the fetters of lust." When the actual moment came, "in an instant ... it was as though the light of confidence flooded into my heart, and all the darkness of doubt was dispelled."

Edith resisted sharing such confidences. *"Secretum meum mihi"*—"This secret belongs to me"—was all she said regarding the reasons for her final step into the Catholic Church. Twenty years passed between her conversion at the age of thirty and her death in 1942. During that time, she never elaborated on either her conversion or the reasons behind her entry into Carmel (although she freely said that the auto-biography of the Carmelite saint Teresa of Avila played a role in both).

When Edith was a child, her family described her as "a book sealed with seven seals." They were accustomed to the fact that she was not self-revealing. But they never suspected she would go over to Catholicism, which they frankly regarded as a "superstitious sect" practiced by the lowest social class. This attitude on their part would make her choice harder for both her unsuspecting family and for Edith, as she worked up the nerve to tell them. The day came, however, when she made her announcement.

"Mother," she said without fanfare, "I am a Catholic."[1] To the daughter's astonishment, Auguste wept. Edith, who had expected anger and possible banishment from home, also wept.

Auguste was bewildered by Edith's decision. To console her, Edith stayed in Breslau for six months, kept up her private tutoring and other professional activities, and participated in family life. "Her mother was the center of her life," said one of Edith's students. "Being ready to care for her always took first place."

Edith even accompanied Auguste to the synagogue, as she had often done in the past. There she prayed alongside her mother, reading the Old Testament psalms from her own missal. These coincided with the psalms used in the synagogue.

Auguste was impressed by her daughter's devout spirit. "I have never seen such prayer as Edith's," she confided in amazement to a friend. Another friend was convinced that "the change that had taken place in Edith, and which lit up her whole being with supernatural radiance, disarmed Frau Stein." Nevertheless, Auguste was not then, nor was she ever, reconciled to Edith's Catholicism.

The immediate blow would have been even greater for the older woman if Edith had immediately pursued her first instinct, to enter the convent. She held off not only to protect her mother from further pain but also because, as a convert, she needed time to settle into her new faith. It soon became apparent that the "settling in" would have to take place in a less distracting environment than the bustling house on Michaelisstrasse.

Shortly after her baptism, Edith placed herself under the spiritual direction of the saintly Canon Joseph Schwind, a priest at the cathedral in Speyer. ("That lady philosopher!" he once exclaimed. "Ten theologians couldn't answer all the questions she asks me.")[2] He arranged a teaching position for her at St. Magdalena's, a Dominican women's school in Speyer. This situation would allow her to live and pray with the nuns while carrying on an active professional life.

Balanced But Busy

Speyer is near Freiburg, close to the French border but far from Breslau. Still, Edith's schedule allowed long vacations at home, which appeased her mother. But not entirely. As the years passed, she began to suspect that Edith would "add insult to injury," in Auguste's words, by entering a convent. And in fact, the setting did allow Edith to live very nearly the life of a nun.

A very busy nun, too. St. Magdalena's consisted of a high school and a teacher's training institute, and Edith taught in both. She also tutored the sisters and novices in preparation for exams, kept up her voluminous correspondence, and devoted many hours to prayer.

She was often in the chapel in the middle of the night, the only time she could find in her packed schedule for sustained prayer. Sometimes she maintained an all-night vigil and then went along to teach her classes in the morning. Her quiet goodness impressed the convent superior. This perceptive woman eventually arranged for

Edith to function as a sort of informal novice mistress, providing spiritual formation for the young sisters.

Edith was available to everyone who wanted her help, and many did. "As to one's relationship with people," she wrote in a letter, "our neighbor's spiritual need transcends *every* commandment. Everything else we do is a means to that end. But love is the end itself, for God is love."[3]

Edith was down-to-earth, too, a trait she combined easily with her intense spirituality. During the school day, she joined the younger girls on the playground for recess, playing forfeits or other games they called for. She persuaded the administration to let her take the girls to the theater for a production of *Hamlet,* an unprecedented outing for the strictly run school.

At Christmas, her room was crammed with gifts she had beautifully wrapped "for everyone in any way connected with her." Edith also rounded up the names and addresses of the poor of the town and delivered Christmas packages to them.

Years later, after Edith's death became known, her former students sent letters about her to the nuns with whom she had lived. She "taught me how to celebrate," one student said in simple tribute. They all remembered her as cheerful, friendly, and "absolutely calm." "She was still and silent," one said. She had become so "perfectly balanced," another said, that you couldn't tell what her temperament was really like.

But a third student injected a note of reality: "Actually, she had an excitable temperament," however well-controlled. This girl recalled one occasion when Edith walked out on the class before the period ended because the students couldn't translate a phrase. "We were left utterly dismayed," the girl said.

They all agreed that "everyone loved her." This was so in spite of the fact that Edith's critical abilities were as sharp as ever. One over-confident student showed up for an oral test certain she would glide through easily. Edith came into the room and began a thorough examination of the material in a way the girl had never experienced. "I failed completely to meet it and grew very silent," she later recalled. "My feeling as I came out was, 'You never met anything as clever as *that* before.'"

Edith knew how to temper honesty with encouragement, although some might have felt she had a slight bias toward honesty. When one girl asked for an assessment of her abilities, Edith told her plainly that she was not so gifted academically as her sisters. "Of course," she added sympathetically, "it is a little oppressive to have such people always at your elbow."

On the other hand, she pointed out, the girl in question had "vigorous reasoning power." She added, "Only you work slowly." Brilliant success, especially in exams, Edith said, would elude her. "But you will always produce something useful."

Edith stayed with the Dominicans for eight years. During all those years, virtually the only criticism leveled at her was that she ate too sparingly and prayed too much. She was not the average convert.

She had searched for truth for fifteen years, beginning with her rejection of faith at the age of fifteen. For Edith at least, that rejection cleared the deck for her to examine all options. When Edith encountered Christianity at Göttingen in her early twenties, she was receptive enough on some deep level to allow the encounter slowly—if subconsciously—to transform her.

Those around her could see from the way she behaved that such a change was under way. She wanted to know the truth not only about

God but also about herself. As she became aware of her faults, she worked hard to fix them.

Well before her conversion, for example, she rooted out her tendency to go on the attack when dealing with challenging people.

> Being right and getting the better of my opponent under any circumstances were no longer essentials for me. Also, although I still had a keen eye for the weaknesses of others, I no longer made it an instrument for striking them at their most vulnerable point, but, rather, for protecting them. Even my tendency to correct others did not affect my new attitude. I had learned that one seldom reforms persons by "telling them the truth." That could benefit them only if they themselves had an earnest desire to improve, and if they accorded one the right to be critical.[4]

She might have reined in her truth telling, as she said, but she never abandoned it.

Jan Nota, a Jesuit priest and friend of Edith, admired the courage that allowed her to speak the truth "to and about others." She managed to do this without condemning or undermining them, a trait he found personally attractive. He acknowledged, however, that it was not "universally appreciated." Even so, her students found her painstaking critiques of their work easy to accept because Edith also took the time to build them up. As one said, she never "squashed" anybody.

It seemed that Edith had arrived at the beginning of her journey of faith equipped with the wisdom one usually accumulates by the end of that journey. To an astonishing measure, this was true. Some of the credit goes to her intellect and some to her sensitive nature, but a great deal of credit goes to her mother.

Auguste embodied many of the best traits of the ideal wife praised in the Old Testament Book of Proverbs (see Pr 31). Day in, day out, this hardworking widow not only provided for her own extended family, "laughing at the days to come," but also helped the poor and needy, shared her wisdom, and watched "the conduct of her household." She certainly didn't eat her food "in idleness." And she never wavered in her faith.

Edith, in her quiet way, saw and noted this. The fact that Auguste trusted her and allowed her to make her own decisions also helped instill in Edith a deep sense of security and self-confidence.

In the long run, Edith didn't need much time to settle into her new faith. However, on the advice of her spiritual director, she continued to postpone her desire to enter the convent. This was not only out of concern for her mother. Her director and others also thought that Edith's intellectual and spiritual gifts deserved a larger arena.

After a few years at Speyer, she gradually returned to her independent intellectual work. She published an essay—entitled "An Investigation of the State"—which was an examination of the political, spiritual, and philosophical elements of national life. In scattered bits of time snatched from her teaching schedule, she translated the letters of Cardinal John Newman and St. Thomas Aquinas' *Quaestiones Disputatae de Veritate* ("Disputed Questions on Truth").

It was the Aquinas, finally, that persuaded her of the inherent goodness of pure intellectual effort. For the first few years after her conversion, Edith thought that loving God meant giving up the things of the world, which, for her, were largely synonymous with the things of the mind.

It was through St. Thomas that it first dawned on me that it was possible to pursue learning in the service of God, and not until then could I bring myself to go on again seriously with intellectual work. I think, even, that the deeper anyone is drawn into God, the more he must go out of himself in this sense, i.e., out into the world, to carry the divine life into it.[5]

Even a contemplative, she said, must not sever her connection with humanity.

Edith was content for the time being to carry the divine life into the little world of St. Magdalena's. However, the familiar back-and-forth pattern of her life was about to reassert itself. As her intellectual work became more widely known, offers began to come in for speaking engagements. In addition to her other duties, she soon found herself on the Catholic lecture circuit.

To all appearances, she was moving even farther away from her goal of the contemplative life. Yet this didn't disturb her. By now she was living according to her guiding principle: "What did not lie in my plans, lay in God's plans."

The topic she was most often asked to deal with in her lectures happened to be one close to her heart: the role of women in the modern world. Her inability to land a job in the male-dominated academic world, her experience growing up in a single-parent home, her own feminism, and her intellectual and spiritual assets, all combined to give her unique insight into this pressing issue.

ELEVEN

LIVING AT THE HAND OF THE LORD

Edith's public role as a lecturer spanned the years from 1927 to 1933. For most of those years, the Nazi party was on the rise in Germany, a fact she occasionally alluded to in her talks. While Edith was delivering her well-crafted, thoughtful speeches on the role of women in society, the bombastic Adolf Hitler was also, occasionally, addressing the same topic at Nazi rallies.

His limited thinking restricted women to "Children, Church, and Kitchen," as a popular Nazi slogan had it. "Women," he said on one occasion, "cannot think logically or reason objectively since they are ruled by their emotions." They were to function, in fact, primarily as breeding machines, and that only if they were of pure "Aryan" stock. Those German women, Hitler said, should have only one goal, the "aim to be mothers."

Hitler wasn't in a position to promote his theories on a national scale until he achieved political power in 1933. Nevertheless, his ideology was in the air, cast in the warm glow of a romanticized motherhood. Edith referred to this in a speech in 1932.

In it, she castigated the "multitude" of "thoughtless people satisfied with hackneyed expressions concerning the *weaker sex* or even the *fair sex*." She singled out romanticists. She faulted them for painting an idealized version of woman as a delicate creature who needed to be sheltered from "the hard facts of life."

"Curiously," Edith said, "this romantic view is connected to that brutal attitude which considers woman merely from the biological point of view.... Gains won during the last decades are being wiped out because of this romanticist ideology, the use of women to bear babies of Aryan stock."[1] The view of women solely as biological entities was a "misinterpretation," she said, that did violence to their spirit.

Even apart from Nazi ideology, society harbored a lingering suspicion that women who worked outside the home violated the "order of nature and grace." God did assign men and women differing roles, Edith agreed, but she emphasized that they shared a "common creativity" evident in all areas of life. When the domestic arena is unable to engage all of a woman's potential, "nature and reason concur that she reach out beyond this circle." In the long run, she said, society could only benefit from women's participation "in the most diverse professional disciplines."

Edith was by no means a radical. "Differences determined by sex do exist," she said. In general, men tend toward the abstract and the impersonal, women toward the concrete, personal, and whole.

Man is "consumed by 'his enterprise'" and finds it difficult to "become involved in other beings and their concerns." Woman is by nature intent on nurturing life, not simply on a biological level—in fact, many women never become mothers—but through her compassionate interest in and encouragement of all who come within her orbit. Edith placed the highest importance on women carrying that attitude into their professional lives.

Married women, however, have a duty first to the home. The danger of work outside the home, said Edith, is that it "will so take over that finally it can make it impossible for her to be the heart of the family and the soul of the home, which must always remain her essential duty." The married woman will normally be "restricted to domestic life at a time when her household duties exact her total energies," especially when she has young children.

On the other hand, the danger of failing to cultivate her own gifts and powers is that she will "lose herself in association with her husband." Further, in her role as his companion and helper, she must see to it that "he is not totally absorbed in his professional work, that he does not permit his humanity to become stunted, and that he does not neglect his family duties as father."

Whether women are working in the world or at home, Edith argued that they need a decent education in order to make their vital contributions to society. In Germany, they had been denied university studies until the early twentieth century. In a talk on the problems of women's education, Edith quoted from the historical record to make her point.

A directive issued by a pedagogical group in 1872, she observed, advocated instruction for women "so that the German husband may not suffer boredom at home." In 1884, a political platform of the Prussian Conservative Party stated: "Every woman actually learns only from the man whom she loves and she learns what the beloved man wants her to learn.... Something can be made [of women] through their brothers, fathers, and older men if they serve these men with warm hearts."

Who was this woman, Edith wanted to know, this "grotesque, petty, middle-class, half-witted caricature of the Old Testament view [of the strong woman]"? Nothing more than an "ornament of the domestic hearth."[2] Edith noted that in the past, this mentality had framed the curricula for high school girls.

A solid education would prepare women for the real world, she said. But Edith was after even more. She delivered her talks primarily to Catholic audiences at conferences and educational association meetings. Here, she could freely address what she considered the essential element of a well-integrated personality: the interior life.

#4a

> Whoever wants to preserve this [nurturing] life continually within herself must nourish it constantly from the source whence it flows without end—from the holy sacraments, above all from the sacrament of love. To have divine love as its inner form, a woman's life must be a eucharistic life. Only in daily, confidential relationship with the Lord in the tabernacle can one forget self, become free of all one's own wishes and pretensions, and have a heart open to all the needs and wants of others.[3]

Edith actually had only one message in these lectures, whether discussing philosophy, education, women's role in society, or anything else. She called this her *ceterum censeo,* a phrase that, in a colloquial sense, means "stubbornly repeated challenge": how one may live at the hand of the Lord, dependent on him alone.

Edith ranged far afield in her talks, but she insisted often on an essential ingredient if women were to fulfill their role in society: the full development of a woman's gifts—spiritual, intellectual, professional, and personal. These, she said, could then be placed at the service of humanity, stamped with the healing touch of an authentic womanly nature.

She made it clear that this can most easily happen when men, too, are operating in conformity with their nature. Since the Fall, however, the sexes are pitted against one another "as they fight for their rights and, in doing so, no longer appear to hear the voices of nature and of God." But it can be different, Edith added, "whenever the power of grace is operative."

Moreover, women can lead the way if they are grounded in an active prayer life. Their innate instincts for healing and wholeness can compensate "for the obvious defects of our masculine Western culture."

In Sight of the Goal

Edith's lectures took her throughout Germany, Austria, and Switzerland. In spite of the demands imposed by travel, she kept up her teaching, writing, and other responsibilities at Speyer. To this, in 1928, she added a small personal compensation. That spring, she went to the Benedictine Abbey of Beuron for a retreat during Holy Week and Easter.

Her spiritual director, Canon Schwind, had recently died of a stroke after fifty-one years as a priest. (He had "never spared himself in his faithfulness" to the priestly ideal, Edith wrote in a tribute to him. "And how he gave you his undivided attention, listening to every word that you said!")

But Edith was not without a spiritual guide for long. At Beuron, she met the Abbot Raphael Walzer, and impressed by his joy as well as his spirituality, she placed herself under his direction. This drew her back to the peaceful Beuron as often as she could manage.

Abbot Walzer was equally impressed with Edith. She was "one of the greatest women of our time," he later wrote of her.

I have seldom met a soul which united so many excellent qualities; and she was simplicity and naturalness personified. She was completely a woman, gentle and even maternal, without ever wanting to "mother" anyone. Gifted with mystical graces in the true sense of the word, she never gave any sign of affectation or sense of superiority. She was simple with simple people, learned with the learned yet without presumption, an enquirer with enquirers, and I would almost like to add, a sinner with sinners.[4]

The abbot, like Canon Schwind before him, dissuaded Edith from entering the convent. Quit teaching at St. Magdalena's, he urged, and move into a more public and possibly more influential life. Exactly what that life might be was not clear, but Edith was warming to the idea.

"Perhaps I shall give up the school," she wrote in a letter late in 1930; "[the talk at] Salzburg drew amazing crowds." In March 1931, she did leave Speyer for good. She didn't have any definite plans, but by then, Edith was accustomed to the mysterious twists and turns of her life. "God knows what he wants of me, and I have no need to worry about it," she wrote to a friend.

Not that Edith allowed herself to drift. She made a concerted effort to apply for teaching positions at the universities of Freiburg and Breslau, but these applications fell through. Now her failure was due not so much to her gender as to her Jewish heritage.

Hitler had published *Mein Kampf*, his bitterly anti-Semitic autobiography, in 1925. Initially the public had ignored his ravings. But Hitler's ideas had gained an audience as Germany and the rest of the world entered the Great Depression.

His speeches and writings denouncing Jews as parasites, cultural saboteurs, and the root cause of economic woe found at least some resonance with impoverished Germans. The sentiments, after all, were not entirely unfamiliar, even if Germany's historic anti-Semitism had been relatively latent in recent years. Increasingly, Jews were under attack in the press and were bypassed for positions of influence in academia and business.

Even in the face of all that, Edith devoted her time to writing and lecturing. As one of the requirements for applying to teach at a university, she completed another dissertation: *Act and Potency.* It examined the relationship between phenomenology and scholasticism, the system of thought advanced by St. Thomas Aquinas. Edith was one of the few people qualified in both systems to undertake such a study.

She also revised and published her two-volume translation of St. Thomas. Her expertise set her apart the following year when she attended a conference on phenomenology and Thomism in Paris. The meeting drew the leading philosophers of Europe, including Jacques Maritain, but it was Edith who took the reins during the discussions. Later, one participant said that she expressed her ideas so clearly, "even in French," that she made a very strong impression on all the scholars who were present.

Edith's job hunt occupied much of 1931, but she spent as much of the year as possible in Breslau. There, the atmosphere at home had become "oppressive" for her sister Rosa. She wanted to follow Edith into Catholicism, but put off her baptism out of respect for their mother. Meanwhile, Auguste's granddaughter, Erika, who lived with the women on Michaelisstrasse, insisted that the household observe an increasingly strict Judaism. The already-kosher kitchen, for example, wasn't kosher enough to suit her.

The stress of hiding her Christian faith while living a more intense

Jewish life made the situation unbearable for Rosa. Edith cheered her up, prayed with her, and occupied Auguste so that Rosa could occasionally slip out of the house to visit church. Then Edith wrote to her friends, "rallying all my troops," she said, to ask their prayers for the situation. (A few years later, Erika emigrated to Palestine and married an orthodox rabbi. She often corresponded often with Edith, helping her with her questions regarding Old Testament texts.)

Finally, with no hope in sight for a university appointment, Edith accepted a position as a lecturer at the Catholic Pedagogical Institute in Munster. Her main responsibility was to construct a Catholic educational theory based on theology and philosophy. She also taught classes on philosophy and pedagogy to the college students there and regarded her work with these young people as her "God-given task."

For this, she was willing to delay her entry into the religious life. But even that level of academic achievement would soon be denied her. Within less than a year, the long arm of the Nazis reached in to remove her from her small sphere of influence.

TWELVE

THE FUTURE BREAKS IN

While at Munster, Edith lived at the Collegium Marianum, a house of studies for religious and college students. Even here, the Nazi influence was evident. One of the students was an ardent fan of *Mein Kampf.* She praised it at length during dinner conversations.

The usually restrained Edith couldn't hide her dislike for the young woman, who also, it happened, smoked constantly. Hitler detested smoking, especially by women, and one day Edith pointed this out sharply to the student. It was a "biting remark," said another woman who witnessed the rebuke.

Edith "liked a little playful malice," said the witness, although, unfortunately, she couldn't remember what Edith said. When Edith later had qualms that she had spoken too sharply, the others assured her they were pleased to see the budding Nazi "catch it for once."

It seemed there was nothing Edith could do, however, about the growing persecution of the Jews. She spoke openly to the students of her Jewish heritage, and they observed that she became "more and more grave" when she thought about her family. As Jews were forced out of business or otherwise restricted, Auguste could barely maintain her lumberyard. Edith didn't complain, a student said, "but it was shattering to see her quiet face, drawn with pain."

Edith had never repudiated her Jewish identity and, in fact, was happy that her relationship to Christ existed "not only in a spiritual sense but in blood terms." "My return to God made me feel Jewish again," she once said. Gradually, Edith was getting a sense of where that understanding might take her.

One night during Lent of 1933, for example, she found herself accidentally locked out of the Marianum. Most of the students were away, so Edith had no luck rousing anyone to answer the bell. A passing professor and his wife stopped to help, recognized her, and invited her back to their house for the night.

Once there, the professor began to tell her of American newspaper reports regarding atrocities committed against Jews, persecution Edith was already aware of. In the middle of the discussion, Edith later wrote, it suddenly became "luminously clear to me that once again God's hand lay heavy on his people, and that the destiny of this people was my own." She kept this intimation hidden from her host, who was unaware of Edith's roots. Although she usually revealed her Jewish identity without hesitation, it seemed to her "that it would be a violation of the law of hospitality to spoil his night's rest" by revealing her status.[1]

She spent the weeks after this conversation thinking "constantly" of what she could do about the rapidly approaching calamity. She decided to bring the urgency of the Nazi threat to the attention of Pope Pius XI. Edith requested a private audience with him, but the Vatican turned her down due to "the pressure of business." She wrote a letter, instead, which her spiritual director, Abbot Raphael, personally delivered to the pope.

Edith asked nothing less than that the pope issue a special encyclical to address the evils of the situation brewing in Germany. Nothing came of this except a return note offering a blessing for the Stein family. Edith later wondered if her letter sometimes came to the pope's mind. "For what I predicted about the future of Catholics in Germany was fulfilled step by step in the following years."

It is possible that the pope did indeed recall his near-brush with Edith. In 1933, the Vatican signed a Concordat with Germany, an agreement designed to protect Catholic rights and institutions there. The Concordat, initiated by the Nazis, was little more than a ruse on Hitler's part to keep the Church quiet while he established his dictatorship. In time, he intended to bring the Church to heel or destroy it.

The Nazis ignored the agreement almost from the start. They hindered religious education, arrested priests and nuns, interfered with Catholic youth groups, and otherwise hampered Catholic ministry. In 1937, Pius XI issued *Mit Brennender Sorge* ("With Burning Anxiety"), the only encyclical ever written in German.

This bitter denunciation of Nazism was smuggled into Germany and read from every Catholic pulpit on March 21, 1937. By that time, however, National Socialism was well entrenched. Also, while the encyclical condemned Nazi errors, it did not mention the plight of German Jews.

Not satisfied, the pope commissioned another encyclical in 1938. *Humani Generis Unitas* ("On the Unity of the Human Race") specifically condemned anti-Semitism, racism, and the exaggerated nationalism of the Nazis. Three Jesuits wrote the letter for the pope, completing it by late 1938. It was an extremely strong statement but exhibited some weaknesses that reflected a historic Catholic bias against Judaism. In short, while the racial anti-Semitism of the Nazis drew condemnation, the religious anti-Semitism familiar to many in this pre-Vatican Council II era passed muster.

At any rate, Pius XI died in February 1939, before he published it.

A draft of the encyclical was found on his desk. His successor, Pope Pius XII, was a man who preferred diplomatic negotiation to confrontation. Perhaps for this reason or perhaps because he recognized the shortcomings of *Humani Generis,* he did not issue the encyclical. In fact, its existence remained hidden for nearly fifty years until discovered by journalists.

All this still lay in the future when Edith tried to bring her concern before Rome. The Vatican's turndown caused her to drop the idea of any further appeal there. Actually, although she felt that the appeal was in keeping with her character, she never thought it was "the real thing" that God was asking of her in regard to "the Jewish question." But neither did she know yet, she said, what her contribution would be.

But she was getting closer to the mark. During the time her request was before the pope, Edith attended the Holy Thursday Mass at the Carmelite convent in Cologne. The priest gave a moving sermon, Edith said.

> But something else deeper than his words was occupying me. I spoke to our Savior and told him that I knew that it was his cross which was now being laid on the Jewish people. Most of them did not understand it; but those who did understand must accept it willingly in the name of all. I wanted to do that, let him only show me how. When the service was over I had an interior conviction that I had been heard. But in what the bearing of the cross was to consist I did not yet know. [2]

A Perspective on Suffering

Dating back to 1918, the cross of Christ had held a central place in Edith's spirituality. That was the year Edith's unbelief had dissolved when she encountered the recently widowed Anna Reinach. Anna was "victorious over the sting of death." The amazed Edith could only attribute this victory to the mystery of Christ's cross and "the divine strength it inspires in those who bear it."

She was drawn increasingly to this cross as the years passed. Her interest was far from morbid, just as she herself was far from gloomy. But she recognized Christ's sacrifice on Golgotha as the central mystery of the Christian faith.

Perhaps it was her own birth on the Jewish Day of Atonement that made her sensitive to the notion of sacrifice in reparation for sin. In the Old Testament many rituals surrounded the Day of Atonement, all designed to rid the Israelites of sin and restore them to God. One of these rituals involved the scapegoat, a living goat symbolically burdened with the sins of the people.

The priest drove this animal out of the Israelite encampment and into the desert, purifying the camp of uncleanness. Christians have long seen the scapegoat as an image of Jesus. "On Golgotha," Edith said, "the true sacrifice of reconciliation was accomplished.... The old sacrifices lost their efficacy."

A long tradition in Catholic theology holds that Christians, in imitation of Christ, can offer themselves to him in voluntary suffering on behalf of sinful humanity. This expiatory suffering, Edith said, is actually effective, canceling "some of the mighty load of human sin." Those Christians who choose this path, however, do so based on a strong relationship with the Lord.

"For by nature, a person flees from suffering. And the mania for suffering caused by a perverse lust for pain differs completely from the desire to suffer in expiation. Such lust is not a spiritual striving," she warned, "but a sensory longing no better than other sensory desires, in fact worse because it is contrary to nature." 3

In contrast, those who have a "predilection for the way of the cross" are characterized by "a strong and pure joy," a trait frequently observed in Edith herself. And because such Christians bind themselves to the cross, they are free of self-interest and able to "descend into the darkest night." "Bound to [the Crucified]," Edith said, "you are omnipresent as he is.... You can be at all fronts, wherever there is grief, in the power of the cross."

It was this sharing in the sufferings of Christ that Edith was getting at when she prayed, at the Holy Thursday Mass, to help bear his cross. She knew that this request would have practical repercussions even if she didn't yet know what they would be. Maybe it would only mean more intense prayer on her part. But she might have suspected, given her premonitions about the extent of the Nazi threat, that it would require something more substantial.

Edith, however, had been training herself for years in a sacrificial lifestyle. She ate little, prayed much, made herself available to all who needed her, never complained when her professional plans failed to pan out. She was already well advanced on "the way of the cross."

In 1930, for example, she had a visit with Edmund Husserl that reflects her sense that while this way of sacrifice was often the higher way, it could carry a price to match. Husserl had converted from Judaism to Christianity as a young man, but had fallen away from the faith. Edith could see that nothing she said about the issue seemed to make any difference. She wrote in a letter to a mutual friend:

I suppose it is good to be able to speak freely to him about ultimate questions. And yet, not only does it increase his own level of responsibility, it also heightens our responsibility for him. Prayer and sacrifice, in my opinion, are much more crucial than anything we can say.... After every meeting with him, I come away convinced of my inability to influence him directly and feeling the urgent necessity of offering some holocaust of my own for him. [4]

Holocaust literally means "something entirely burned up," a total offering. At the time, of course, Edith could not know that this word would be applied to Hitler's attempt to eradicate the Jews. Nor that she would be a victim of that Holocaust. She simply chose that unusual word to describe her sense that some situations demand a wholehearted, sacrificial response.

Husserl's plight was one such situation. So, too, on a different scale, was the terrible persecution of the Jews just beginning. In both cases, Edith made it clear that she stood ready to offer herself to the fullest extent necessary in order to help alleviate the sufferings of others.

Glad Agreement

On April 20, 1933, the future broke in on Edith in an ominous manner. The Nazis had recently passed a law dismissing Jews from government and public positions. When Edith returned to Munster from Easter vacation, the administrator told her that because of her Jewish heritage she could no longer teach at the Institute.

He suggested that she work quietly at the Marianum until the autumn. By then, he hoped, they'd have a better idea how intent the government was on enforcing the law. "If I can't go on here," Edith replied with sharp insight, "then there is nothing possible for me anymore in Germany." She also understood, but didn't say, that since the Institute was Catholic, "its days were doubtless numbered."

"I was almost relieved to find myself now involved in the common fate of my people," Edith said. And now the thought dawned: With her professional opportunities severely restricted, was it "not time at last to enter Carmel?" From the moment of her baptism in 1921, Edith had felt a strong tug in that direction. "Our Lord was keeping something for me in Carmel that I could find only there."

She had deferred the fulfillment of her dream under the advice of her spiritual directors. Now there was nothing to stop her. Her career in Germany was over, and although she could go abroad to work, the idea didn't appeal to her. As for her mother, wouldn't she be happier to have her in a convent in Germany rather than living in another country? (As to that, Auguste would have preferred she go abroad, but Edith didn't know that at the time.)

With the blessing of Abbot Raphael, Edith applied to the Carmelite convent in Cologne. Her age was against her (she was forty-two), her Jewish identity could threaten the security of the convent, and she had no money to offer as a dowry. Nevertheless, the superior met and approved of Edith and agreed to put her petition before the other women in the Carmel. Edith met these nuns for a brief interview on June 18, but then left the convent the next day to wait while they voted on her admission.

The very next day, the telegram arrived: "Glad agreement. Greetings. Carmel."

THIRTEEN

CARMEL: A PERFECT FIT

Edith knew that the last and biggest hurdle to her departure for Carmel lay in Breslau. She sent the family a letter telling them that some sisters in Cologne had accepted her. They assumed she had found another professional position and sent their congratulations back. She let that impression stand. In mid-August, she returned for two final months with her relatives on Michaelisstrasse.

As soon as she arrived in Breslau, Edith told Rosa her plans. Rosa was Catholic in spirit if not yet in fact, but this possibility had never occurred "even to her." If Rosa was amazed by such a turn of events, Edith knew the disclosure to her mother would be as difficult as she anticipated.

Auguste was gloomy over national events; she never knew "there could be such wicked people" in the world. "But she came to life again when I arrived," Edith said. Her sense of humor revived, helped by the opportunity to unburden herself to her daughter.

Each evening, after a day at the lumberyard, she sat by Edith's desk, knitting in hand, eager to chat. Edith, for her part, took advantage of these moments to collect her mother's memories for her book, *Life in a Jewish Family.* "It was evident that being together like this" was doing her mother good, Edith said. "But all the time I had to think, 'If you but knew!'"

Finally, the moment came.

119

On the first Sunday in September I was alone at home with my mother. She was sitting at the window with her knitting, and I was beside her. Suddenly, the long-expected question came: "What are you going to do with the sisters in Cologne?" "Live with them." Then came a desperate effort to deter me. My mother did not stop working. Her wool got into a tangle. She tried with trembling hands to unravel it, and I helped her, while we carried on our discussion. There was no more peace from now on. A cloud hung over the whole house.[1]

Over the following weeks, Auguste made occasional attempts to discourage Edith, lapsing into "silent despair" each time she encountered anew Edith's quiet determination. Her siblings never tried to sway her, deeming it pointless to try.

Privately, Edith did reevaluate the pros and cons of her choice. "The decision was so difficult that no one could say with certainty whether this road or that was the right one.... I had to take the step entirely in the darkness of faith."

Finally, her last full day at home arrived. It happened to be Edith's birthday, October 12, as well as the Jewish Feast of Tabernacles. Edith accompanied her mother to the synagogue for the service.

At Auguste's insistence, they walked home afterwards—"three quarters of an hour and she was eighty-four!" On the way, she asked if Edith thought it was possible for a Jew to be pious. When Edith said, "Of course," her mother exclaimed: "I don't want to say anything against [Jesus]. He may have been a very good man. But why did he make himself God?"

The afternoon and evening passed in a flurry of guests who had come to see Edith off. It was hard, she said, when everyone finally left.

"In the end, my mother and I were alone in the room; my sisters were still clearing away and washing up. Then she hid her face in her hands and began to weep. I stood behind her chair and laid her snowy gray head on my breast. We stayed so for a long while."

Finally, Edith took her upstairs, helped her get ready for bed, and then sat on the edge of her bed until Auguste sent her away. "I think neither of us had any rest that night," Edith said.

It was no better in the morning. Auguste tried to take some coffee "but soon pushed the cup away and began to weep.... I went to her again," Edith said, "and held her in my arms until it was time to go."

When the actual parting came, Auguste embraced and kissed Edith "very tenderly." They never saw each other again. Edith's sisters, Else and Rosa, took her to the station, put her on the train, and at last, Edith said, "what I hardly dared to hope for was real."

There was no great rush of happiness, however. "All that lay behind me," she later recalled, "was too terrible for that. But I was in deep peace—in the haven of the divine will."

Carmel at Last

The Discalced Carmelite Order is the more austere of the two Carmelite religious orders. Both claim continuity with hermits who settled on Mount Carmel in ancient times. In the sixteenth century, St. Teresa of Avila and St. John of the Cross sought to counter the laxity that had gradually set in, so they introduced a return to the original, ascetic rule. Those who accepted that reform became known as the Discalced (shoeless) Carmelites. Edith was joining the Discalced Order.

The Carmelite life centers on prayer and penance, and the convents observe strict poverty. Even those familiar with Carmelite spirituality, Edith's novice mistress observed, "can scarcely avoid shrinking when for the first time they begin to breathe the dry air of Carmel." But to this life, Abbot Raphael said, Edith "ran ... like a child into its mother's arms, blithe and singing." She never regretted it, and she never looked back.

In fact, others noted that she seemed to grow younger and happier as she settled into the new routine. Hedwig Conrad-Martius, her old friend, said that after a time, Edith had an "aura of childlike happiness and contentment" that was "absolutely charming."

However, the transition was not easy. Edith was not accustomed to a heavily regulated schedule. And as a professional, she had not often dealt with the tasks of ordinary domestic life. Further, none of her fellow nuns knew that she was a well-respected intellectual in the Church and the academic world. This indifference toward her reputation was intentional and meant to encourage humility in her: Edith was to be just another postulant.

" 'Does she sew nicely?' The searching question came from one of the older sisters," the novice mistress reported, "and it helps one to appreciate the standard of values applied to the new postulant. Unfortunately, Edith sewed very badly; worse, it was positively painful watching her trying to do housework, at which she was so clumsy and unskilled." [2]

But Edith went at everything with a good will and genuine humility and said the experience was good for someone "who had been excessively praised all her life." The other nuns loved her. She had a "disarming friendliness" and a ready wit, her novice mistress said, and knew how to tell a story so that even the smallest incident became "a thrilling adventure." Along with these appealing traits, Edith also "had a great inclination towards the seclusion which is the true life of Carmel."

After a six-month probationary period, Edith received the habit of the order in a ceremony on April 15, 1934. At that time, she also took the name Teresa Benedicta a Cruce: "Teresa," in honor of St. Teresa of Avila; "Benedicta," in honor of St. Benedict and the Benedictines whose spirit, at Beuron, impressed her so much; "a Cruce"—of the Cross—in recognition of her devotion to the cross of Christ. From then on she was known in the religious life as Benedicta.

The sisters were prepared for a crowd but were amazed at the throngs that descended on the convent for the ceremony—philosophers, professors, former students, and representatives of many religious orders. Husserl regretted he was unable to attend and felt he should have been there as her "father." "Everything in her is utterly genuine," he said, "otherwise I should say that this step was romanticism. But—deep down in Jews is radicalism and love faithful unto martyrdom." [3]

Edith's brothers and sisters sent greetings, but none of them attended. Auguste was not informed of the ceremony, and it would have aroused her suspicions if Rosa had made the trip. Nevertheless, the event "was an overwhelming testimony to the high esteem and love which Edith had enjoyed in the world," her novice mistress said.

The rhythm of convent life absorbed Edith for the following year of her novitiate. The women rose at 4:30 each morning and retired at 9:00 in the evening, spending much of the time in between at prayer. Some of this was intercessory. When a friend wrote requesting prayer, Edith wrote back to assure her that "such requests are not out of the ordinary for us."

Each day's mail or knock at the door brought similar pleas. "After all, it is our profession to pray, and many people rely on that.... It is a real source of embarrassment for us when people credit us with special effectiveness in prayer, or with holiness.... Despite that, it does seem that the Lord gladly helps those who turn to us."[4] She added that the person asking for prayer also had to "be sensible" and do his part, whatever that might be.

Edith wrote to another friend that there was very little opportunity for scholarly work. However, from the moment Edith entered, the prioress had asked her to take on occasional writing projects. Initially, these were short biographies of saints for feast days or translations of texts into Latin for use at Mass. Later, she would take on more intellectual, philosophical writing.

Edith also kept up her correspondence and met with visitors in the "speakroom," where she, like all the nuns, talked with her guests from behind a grate. Come visit me, she wrote to Fritz Kaufmann. "You were mistaken in thinking that you had to take leave of me [when I entered the cloister].... All my visitors who have been close to me have assured me that after a few minutes they are no longer aware of the grates because the spirit moves through them without hindrance."[5]

The only personal request Edith made when entering Carmel was that she be allowed to write to her mother weekly, a mutual correspondence that the two had faithfully practiced for years. The prioress agreed, and each week Edith's letter dutifully went off. But for the first few years Auguste never replied.

Rosa answered in her stead, keeping Edith abreast of family news. From Rosa and others, Edith learned that there was "much bitterness" in her mother. "It makes me sad," Edith wrote to Erna without elaborating, "to see what caricatures she has thought up—not only about [the] faith and about life in our Order, but also about my personal motives."

On Easter Sunday 1935, Edith made her profession of temporary vows. It would be another three years, according to the rule of the Order, before she would make her final vows, which would be permanent. According to custom, the ceremony took place privately with only her fellow nuns in attendance.

Not long after, Edith wrote to her mother to describe the occasion. To her amazement, Auguste wrote back offering her best wishes. There was no explanation for her change of attitude. After that, all Rosa's letters from home contained a few lines from her mother.

The ongoing political turmoil in Germany overshadowed the intense joy Edith felt upon taking her vows. Her foreboding was well-founded. In September of 1935, the Nazis enacted the infamous Nuremberg Laws stripping Jews of the vote and turning them into second-class citizens. Other provisions of the law that forbade Jews to marry Aryans also instituted a classification system denoting degrees of Jewishness. These were based on the Jewish blood of one's grandparents, and each degree carried certain rights and restrictions.

Well before these laws went into effect, Edith had a visit from the wife of a local teacher. The woman assured her that in Carmel, at least, Edith would be safe from the Nazis. "No, I don't think so," Edith replied. "I am sure that they will come and search me out here. In any case, I should not count upon being left here in peace."

Safely Home

At the direction of her superiors, Edith spent much of 1935 and into the summer of 1936 working on her uncompleted thesis, *Act and*

Potency. This manuscript, an investigation of phenomenology, Catholic tradition, and the links between the two, moved beyond philosophical thinking into the realm of faith. In a sense, Roman Ingarden later said, Edith had left philosophy behind. She re-titled the work *Finite and Eternal Being,* but couldn't get it published because of her Jewish blood. "I think it will have to be a posthumous work," she said, simply.

At any rate, her scholarly efforts took a backseat to a development of a more personal nature. Auguste had been diagnosed with cancer of the stomach and was failing fast. Her suffering increased over the summer until finally she was bedridden.

On September 14, 1936, the Feast of the Exaltation of the Cross, the nuns of the Cologne Carmel gathered at dawn for their yearly renewal of vows. After the ceremony, Edith told one of the sisters what she had experienced as she waited to make her recommitment: "My mother was beside me. I felt her presence quite distinctly."

A telegram later that day informed Edith that her mother had died. The time of death coincided with Edith's renewal of vows.

Edith quickly dispelled rumors that her mother had converted to Christianity at the end. Auguste's Jewish faith was "her last support in her hard struggle with death," Edith wrote to a friend. "I am confident that she has found a most merciful judge, and that she is now my most faithful helper on my own journey towards my homeland."[6]

FOURTEEN

No Longer Safe

Edith's sense that not even the walls of Carmel could guarantee safety received distressing proof from an unexpected quarter. A few months after the Spanish Civil War erupted in 1936, soldiers murdered three Discalced Carmelite sisters in Gaudalajara. The women were shot to death specifically because they were nuns.

"So far we still live in deep peace, entirely unmolested within our convent walls," Edith wrote in a letter. "But the fate of our Spanish sisters tells us, all the same, what we must be prepared for. And when such profound upheaval takes place in such close proximity, it is a salutary warning."[1]

To all appearances, life rolled on peacefully enough in Carmel, but Edith's letters occasionally reflect her unease. Auguste's will, for example, specified that the two sisters remaining at home—Rosa and Frieda—were to maintain the house on Michaelisstrasse as a base for the whole family. But they could only do that "as long as the present circumstances allow," Edith wrote in a veiled reference to Nazi restrictions on the rights of Jews.

It didn't look as though the "circumstances" were going to get better. By the late 1930s and into the 1940s, blatantly discriminatory laws banned Jews from such disparate occupations as medicine, accounting, dentistry, editing, and acting as tour guides. Jewish lawyers were disbarred. Jews couldn't serve in the military.

Nazi courts empowered "law enforcement" officials to confiscate Jewish property and businesses and then turn them over to Aryans. Jewish children were ousted from the school system. Jewish men and women had to add "Israel" or "Sarah" to their names.

The laws became so restrictive as to be ludicrous. Jews couldn't own pets. They were banned from fishing and playing sports. In one village, they were barred from using the communal bull to impregnate their cows. In the parks of Berlin, Jews could sit only on yellow benches designated for their use.

At the same time, the Nazis were closing all religious schools, such as St. Magdalena's at Speyer. The religious who taught in these institutions were turned out of their convents and monasteries. Edith wrote to a nun in this situation:

Certainly, it is difficult to live outside the convent and without [having] the Blessed Sacrament [reserved in the house]. But God is within us after all, the entire Blessed Trinity, if we can but understand how to build within ourselves a well-locked cell and withdraw there as often as possible, then we will lack nothing anywhere in the world. That, after all, is how the priests and religious in prison must help themselves. For those who grasp this it becomes a time of great grace. [2]

For the most part, however, the events of the day were "certainly things one cannot write about," as Edith phrased it, for fear the correspondence would fall into Nazi hands. "Much has to remain unsaid." Edith's comments generally strayed no farther than the observation that "everything is disintegrating and changing."

She was somewhat more explicit when, in reference to her family, she wrote: "They are all very intimidated out there, for they can never really know whom they might still expect to associate with them." And the death of an acquaintance prompted her to observe that "today, more than ever, one does not begrudge anyone eternal rest and is grateful for all who have escaped the sufferings of these times."

Glimmers of Light

These years of turmoil were not without consolation. Even Auguste's death brought Edith some comfort. For one thing, she was now out of reach of the Nazis. For another, she was "no longer waiting in vain" for Edith to return home, a hope Auguste cherished to the end. "She is at peace and understands everything."

Presumably, then, from the perspective of eternity, Auguste understood the speed with which Rosa applied for baptism. Within a few months of her mother's death, Rosa traveled to Cologne for her first reunion with Edith in three years. More important, she would then receive baptism on Christmas Eve at the church of Hohenlind near the Carmel. Edith couldn't leave the cloister itself for the ceremony, but she would meet with her sister in the speakroom to give final instruction in the faith.

The day before Rosa arrived, an accident threatened to undo the carefully laid plans. While groping for a light switch in the dark, Edith fell down the stairs and broke her left hand and left foot. The doctor came, examined the patient, and sent her off to the hospital for x-rays and casts.

The mishap turned out to be a blessing in disguise. Edith was confined to the hospital, where she could talk with Rosa face-to-face rather than through the grille as at the convent. Even better, when the doctor released Edith from the hospital on December 24, the prioress allowed her to stop at Hohenlind to attend Rosa's baptism.

In a way, the ceremony marked the beginning of the end for the two sisters. Their common faith now bound them more closely than ever and set them, together, on the final leg of their journey. Within five years, Rosa and Edith, who stood together at the baptismal font in Hohenlind, would stand together in the gas chamber at Auschwitz.

In the interim, their affection for one another, already deep, grew even stronger. Rosa returned to Breslau, but "in her heart," Edith said, "she is here with us always. And we on our part are doing whatever we can to make her realize that she is one of us."

In April of 1938, the hour at last arrived when Edith herself became irrevocably one with the Carmelites. On Holy Thursday, she made her final profession of vows. At the time, Husserl lay desperately ill with pleurisy. Edith had stayed in close contact with him over the years and now had a sense that his death would coincide with her final profession.

"You see," she wrote in a letter, "I considered that it would be a coincidence similar to the one that occurred when my mother died at the hour we made our renewal of vows. You will not think of me as being so confident of the efficacy of my prayers.... No, I am merely convinced that God calls no one for one's own sake alone. Every time he does call anyone, he's lavish in offering proofs of his love." [3] As it turned out, Husserl would die within a week of Edith's profession, reconciled to the faith.

When the Master awoke on Good Friday, he exclaimed, "Good Friday! What a wonderful day. Christ has forgiven us everything."

Later in the day, he said: "I have fervently prayed to God to let me die and he has given his consent. I find it a great disappointment that I am still alive. God is good—yes, good but so incomprehensible. It is a heavy trial for me. Light and darkness … deep darkness, and again light."

He then became silent until the moment of his death a few days later on April 27. "Oh! I have seen something so wonderful," he said. "Quick, write it down."[4] And then, before he could say anything more, he died.

A Gathering Gloom

"I do not know if I can ever write anything major again," Edith observed late in 1937. "For the present, entirely different tasks seem to await me."

Well into 1938, Edith's duties at Carmel absorbed most of her time. She tended the sick in the infirmary throughout the fall of 1937 and then was appointed as portress. All outside contact with the world passed through this position, from phone calls to ordering supplies to announcing and providing for guests. "I take what comes," she said, "and ask only that I be granted the necessary abilities to accomplish whatever is required of me."

Against this purposeful background, Edith's letters again reflected the growing tensions in the world outside. She spoke of the efforts of various family members to emigrate.

"If only they knew where to go!" she wrote. "They are all very worried." "My brothers and sisters and their children … are in great trouble," she told another friend. "I must pray that they find a home on earth."

The horrors of *Kristallnacht*—the "Night of Broken Glass"—added new urgency to Edith's concern. On November 7, 1938, a German Jewish refugee in Paris shot a German diplomat there. The diplomat died shortly after. In retaliation, the Nazis orchestrated a pogrom against the Jews in Germany and told the police not to interfere.

On the evening of November 9 and into the next day, Nazi storm troopers led mobs in setting fire to at least a thousand synagogues. They smashed windows of Jewish stores and looted everything at hand, from jewelry to groceries. As the violence spread, crowds invaded and ransacked Jewish homes and killed more than ninety Jews. Troops arrested some thirty thousand Jewish men, many of whom ended up in concentration camps.

Edith's family escaped the devastation of *Kristallnacht,* but the pogrom spurred most of them to flee the country. Edith's brother Arno had left for the United States a month before, "just in the nick of time." His wife and two of their children were already there, but their son Wolfgang was in a concentration camp. He was released and allowed to emigrate.

Arno's retarded daughter Eva, however, had been unable to pass the literacy tests demanded by officials at the American consulate in Berlin. Fearing she would be unemployable, they denied her application. Eva, in her mid-twenties but with the mental ability of an eight-year-old, stayed behind in a boarding house, cared for by various relatives and friends. (Eva died in Theresienstadt concentration camp in 1943.)

Edith's sister Elsa and her husband and children fled to South America. Hans Biberstein, in America scouting out job possibilities, landed a teaching position at Columbia University's medical school in New York. German authorities allowed his wife, Erna, and their two teenage children to join him. The Steins' cousin, Richard Courant, left for a job at New York University. Only Edith's sisters Frieda and Rosa, as well as their oldest brother Paul and his wife Trude, were unable to arrange emigration.

Edith herself was now in danger. Worse, from her point of view, was the threat her presence, as a Jew, posed to the Carmel in Cologne. In the past, she had proposed a transfer to a Carmel in Palestine, but her superiors wouldn't consider it.

Now, in the shadow of *Kristallnacht*, everyone agreed that Edith was no longer safe. Since Palestine had recently closed its borders to German Jews, the prioress wrote to the Carmel at Echt in Holland. Edith needed "a change of air," the prioress said delicately. The nuns at Echt understood immediately and invited Edith to join them.

A New Home

On the night of December 31, 1938, Dr. Paul Strerath, a friend of the Cologne community, drove Edith into Holland under cover of darkness. The trip was uneventful, and Edith soon settled into the new surroundings. Humanly speaking, though, there was "no consolation" to ease the departure from Cologne. But "he who lays the cross [on us] understands well how to make the burden light and sweet," she said. "Surely it is God's will that has led me here. And that is the most secure port of peace."[5]

The nuns loved her from the start—she was "serious and cheerful," could "laugh heartily and was always glad to tell stories about her interesting life." They did notice, however, her all-thumbs approach to housework. She was a hard worker, they later recalled, "ever ready to help … [but] she [often] got in the way through over-eagerness, because with all her good will she could never make a thorough job of anything practical."

Initially, she spent her time working on the index for *Finite and Eternal Being.* But within a few weeks of arriving at Echt, Edith wrote to Cologne to ask if someone could bring her the manuscript for her book *Life in a Jewish Family.* She had left it behind fearing that it might be confiscated if she were searched at the border. Given the subject matter, transporting the manuscript would be risky for anybody, Jew or non-Jew.

"There was indeed one intrepid friend, a young Marianhill missionary, Fr. Rhabanus, C.M.M., who declared himself prepared for such an adventure," the translator of *Life in a Jewish Family* wrote in an afterword to the book. "His car was stopped at the Dutch border for a search. The official noted the manuscript, hefted the bulky pack, turned to a few random pages for a quick glance, and then returned it to the priest with the verdict: 'Looks like your doctoral dissertation, eh!' Not a word to correct this opinion, of course, and thus the precious manuscript made its entry into Holland." [6]

Edith never did much more work on *Life in a Jewish Family,* but she evidently considered it of some value. After the Nazis invaded Holland in 1940, she knew that a book about Jews could endanger the convent if the authorities ever found it. But rather than destroy it, she wrapped up the book and buried it in the ground within the monastery enclosure.

Fearing that moisture and dirt would damage it, she unearthed it after three months. At that point, another nun, "taking pity on her helplessness," retrieved it from Edith and hid it. Thus it survived the war.

Of greater concern to Edith as 1939 pressed on was the fate of her sister Rosa. Frieda and Rosa sold the house on Michaelisstrasse, and Frieda went to a government home for Jewish women. The Nazis later deported her to the camp at Theresienstadt, where she died in 1942.

Rosa's heart, however, was with the Carmelites. Unable to get permission to cross into Holland, she eventually answered a newspaper ad from a Belgian woman who was trying to attract members for a new religious order. After the sale of the house, Rosa had stored what was left of the Stein household furniture and goods in a facility near the Belgian border. She then brought it with her into Belgium only to discover that the woman who had placed the ad was a con-artist.

Alerted to this turn of events, Edith put her many friends to work and eventually secured a passport for Rosa to enter Holland. She joined Edith there in the summer of 1940, minus all her possessions. The authorities had forced her to leave her valuables behind and allowed the con-artist to claim everything. Rosa joked that she had become "detached from all her worldly goods at one swoop."

Friends and family heaved a sigh of relief. The Nazis had taken over Holland, but it seemed that Rosa and Edith, tucked away in the Carmel at Echt, were safe. And so they were, for two more years.

FIFTEEN

THE WORLD IN FLAMES

Edith may have been the least domestically inclined of the eighteen nuns at Echt, but the convent was large and rural and could survive only if everyone pitched in. She worked as the portress, was in charge of the dining room, helped with the laundry, harvested and preserved fruit—an overabundance in 1939, she pointed out—and cleaned the house. And then, she said, "after ... seven hours of prayer there is little time left" for writing.

But she did write, tapping into the intense powers of concentration she had honed during her academic career. "I don't use extraordinary means to prolong my workday," she once told someone. "I do as much as I can. The ability to accomplish increases noticeably in proportion to the number of things that must be done.... Heaven is expert at economy."[1]

Initially, the prioress had asked Edith to write some short devotional works for various occasions. If the nuns were hoping for consoling pieties to sustain them during cataclysmic times, Edith failed to deliver. In September 1939, she wrote a meditation for the annual renewal of vows that coincided with the Feast of the Elevation of the Holy Cross.

"Will you remain faithful to the Crucified?" she asked. "Consider carefully! The world is in flames, the battle between Christ and the

Antichrist has broken into the open. If you decide for Christ, it could cost you your life. Carefully consider what you promise. Taking and renewing vows is a dreadfully serious business."[2]

Most of the nuns Edith addressed were older than she and well schooled in the life of sacrifice. But tough times demanded tough words, and Edith was not one to flinch.

Two years later, on the same feast day, she returned to the same topic. The nuns were restricted to the cloister, but "God did not pledge to leave [them] within the walls of the enclosure forever." The Nazis might drive them "out into the street," as had already happened to Carmelites in Germany and Luxembourg.

In that case, "the Lord will send his angels to encamp themselves around us....We may ask that this experience be spared us, but only with the solemn and honestly intended addition: Not mine, but your will be done!"[3]

For Edith, everything hinged on submission to the will of God "because this was the content of the Savior's life." "The greatest hindrances do not come from without but lie within us," she wrote, in the human inclination to resist God. Nevertheless, she reminded the nuns, those who did obey him had an essential role to play in the tragedy then unfolding across Europe.

The more an era is engulfed in the night of sin and estrangement from God the more it needs souls united to God. And God does not permit a deficiency. The greatest figures of prophecy and sanctity step forth out of the darkest night. But for the most part the formative stream of the mystical life remains invisible. Certainly the decisive turning points in world history are substantially co-determined by souls whom no history book ever mentions. And we will only find out about those souls to whom we owe those decisive turning points in our personal lives on the day when all that is hidden is revealed.[4]

The Noose Tightens

These occasional pieces Edith produced gave way, in the summer of 1941, to an in-depth study of St. John of the Cross. The prioress excused Edith from all household chores and asked that she spend the additional time preparing a book in honor of the four-hundredth anniversary of St. John's birth. "I live almost constantly immersed in thoughts about our Holy Father John," she said in a letter, a "great grace" in the darkening times.

She called the book *The Science of the Cross*. Primarily an exposition of St. John's theology, it was also a personal disclosure of Edith's own understanding of life lived under the sign of the cross.

Increasingly, her own circumstances reflected the material she studied. The Nazis announced in December 1941 that all non-Aryan Germans in Holland were considered stateless and must report to the authorities to register for deportation. Edith and Rosa complied.

Efforts were already beginning, however, to transfer Edith to a Carmel in Switzerland and Rosa to a religious community near it. (The Carmel was overcrowded and unable to accept both women.) Meanwhile, they stayed on at Echt. "I am satisfied with everything," Edith said. "A *scientia crucis* [knowledge of the cross] can be gained only when one comes to feel the Cross radically. I have been convinced of that from the first moment and have said, from my heart: *Ave, Crux, spes unica!* [Hail, Cross, our only hope]!"[5]

Edith followed her daily routine calmly even when, early in 1942, the Gestapo—the dreaded Nazi secret police—summoned Edith and Rosa to Maastricht for interrogation. The Dutch Carmelite provincial, Fr.Cornelius Lennissen, went first and tried to persuade the Nazis that strict laws of enclosure prevented Edith, at least, from appearing. The Germans were not moved.

The two sisters went in person, but when Edith entered the Gestapo office she greeted the Nazis with an emphatic "Praised be Jesus Christ!" The men "simply looked up and made no answer." Edith later told her prioress that she felt "driven" to offer the greeting even though to do so was obviously risky. "She saw quite clearly," the prioress said, "that this was no mere question of diplomacy but was part of the eternal struggle" between Jesus and Satan.[6]

Other summonses came, including a trip to Gestapo headquarters in Amsterdam, where Rosa and Edith filled out endless forms to no apparent purpose. Both women were prepared for deportation, at the minimum. Neither knew, of course, the actual scope of the Nazi plans then underway.

In January 1942, while Edith was hard at work on *The Science of the Cross,* Nazi leaders were hard at work laying the plans for the extermination of the Jews. Until that time, at least in theory, Jews could emigrate from German-occupied territories. But sometime in 1941—the Nazis were careful to leave no written records—Hitler decided on the more radical plan of genocide.

Rheinhard Heydrich, head of Reich Security, presented this "Final Solution" to other Nazi leaders at the Wannsee Conference in the suburbs of Berlin on January 20, 1942. "In place of emigration, the evacuation of the Jews has now emerged," he said. "Evacuation" was a euphemism for annihilation. The ensuing discussion over the best methods for wholesale murder made that clear.

Edith was ready for whatever fate the Nazis might send her. In 1939, shortly after arriving at Echt, she had offered herself to God as a sacrifice of expiation "for true peace that the reign of Antichrist might collapse."

Her final testament, written that same year, made her offering explicit.

I joyfully accept in advance the death God has appointed for me.... May the Lord accept my life and death for the honor and glory of his name, for the needs of his holy Church—especially for the preservation, sanctification, and final perfecting of our holy Order … for the Jewish people, that the Lord may be received by his own and his Kingdom come in glory, for the deliverance of Germany and peace throughout the world, and finally, for all my relations living and dead and all whom God has given me: may none of them be lost.[7]

Her thinking reflected the affinity she felt for the biblical Esther, the Jewish queen who had offered her life to save her people. "Esther had been chosen from her people specifically to intercede for them before the King," Edith wrote. "I am a little Esther, poor and powerless, but the King who has chosen me is infinitely great and merciful. And that is a profound consolation."[8]

Edith may have been prepared for death, but she didn't intend to put herself in harm's way. "For months," she wrote to the sisters at Cologne, "I have been wearing next to my heart a piece of paper with the twenty-third verse of Matthew 10 written on it." (The text reads: "When they persecute you in one town, flee to the next. I solemnly assure you, you will not have covered the towns of Israel before the Son of Man comes.")

She followed the progress of the emigration applications and wrote to friends in Switzerland who might be able to speed up the process. Various permissions were necessary—from government and Church officials—and the difficulty of wartime communications, coupled with bureaucratic red tape, slowed the process dramatically. In July 1942, however, the situation resolved itself. A confrontation between the Nazis and Dutch Christians decided Edith and Rosa's fate once and for all.

The Churches Respond

On July 11, with deportations underway, Catholic and Protestant clergy issued a formal protest regarding the treatment of the Jews. In a telegram to Reichskommissar Seyss-Inquart, they condemned the measures that restricted Jews from public life. These measures ranged from the dismissal of Jewish children from public schools to severe restrictions on employment to requiring Jews to wear the yellow Star of David in public.

Now, the churchmen said, they had learned "with horror" of the deportations. Not only would these uprootings cause immeasurable suffering, they were also "contrary to the deepest convictions of the Dutch people." They petitioned the Nazis "urgently" to cancel the deportations. In conclusion, the clergy pointed out that Christians of Jewish descent would be cut off from the life of the Church under the Nazi measures.

The authorities responded by deciding they would not deport

Jewish Christians who had been baptized before January 1941. Catholic church leaders, not satisfied, drafted a   pastoral letter condemning Nazi actions. Seyss-Inquart got wind of this at the last minute and demanded they desist. The Catholic bishops refused.

On July 26, priests throughout the Netherlands read the letter from their pulpits. After stating that the Nazis were inflicting great harm on the Jews, the letter stressed the culpability of all people for the looming disaster.

> Everything around us points toward divine judgment. But thank God, for us it is not too late. We can still avert that judgment if we recognize that time of grace, if we only see the path to peace. And that is none other than a return to God.... All human remedies are now in vain—God is our only hope.

The letter called upon Christians to examine themselves "in a spirit of deep repentance and humility."

> For do we not share the blame for the catastrophes we are enduring? Have we always sought the kingdom of God and his justice? Have we always fulfilled our duties towards our neighbors, treating them justly and loving them? Have we not perhaps harbored feelings of gnawing hatred and bitterness? Have we always sought our refuge in God, our heavenly Father? [9]

The Nazis, enraged, retaliated. The order came swiftly: "Since the Catholic bishops interfered in this matter which was not their concern, the entire population of Catholic Jews are to be deported this week. No interventions are to be considered." In the following few days, the

Nazis rounded up approximately seven hundred Catholic Jews.

On August 2, at 5:00 in the afternoon, Edith had just joined the other nuns in the chapel for meditation.[10] Sharp knocks at the parlor door drew the prioress to the speakroom, where she found two Nazi officers. They demanded to speak to Edith and Rosa. Thinking they had come to discuss the exit permits for Switzerland, the prioress sent Edith to them and then stood at the door to listen to the conversation.

"To my horror," she later wrote, the men turned out to be SS officers whom she heard give Edith five minutes to leave the convent. Then she heard Edith reply, "I cannot. We are strictly enclosed."

"Get this [grille] out of the way," one of the SS officers said, "and come out."

"You must show me how to do it first," Edith said.

"Call your superior," they countered.

At this point, the prioress stepped forward to argue for more time as Edith hurried out to throw some things together. The men refused to negotiate with the prioress and told her to give Edith "a blanket, mug, spoon, and three days' rations." When she again pleaded for time, the SS spokesman said, "You don't need me to tell you what will happen to you and your convent if you refuse to send Sr. Stein out."

Amazingly, she kept up the fight and asked for a half hour "at least." They refused. Finally the prioress capitulated: "If we must give way to force, we do so in the name of God."

Edith, meanwhile, had slipped back into the chapel where she knelt in brief prayer. "Please pray, Sisters," she said to the nuns as she hurried out to put her things together. Some of the nuns followed to help pack, some bundled scraps of food together, and within minutes, Edith was at the enclosure door. She asked the prioress to write quickly for the entry permits to Switzerland, and then she and Rosa were on the street. The prioress could hear Edith "explaining her plans for leaving the country to the SS men" as they walked off.

A crowd had gathered, distraught to see the women led away. Rosa, in particular, was "deeply loved and admired by the local people," a nun said. She had visited the sick, attended funerals, shopped, and otherwise represented the convent "on the outside."

A witness reported that as they walked to the corner and the waiting van, Edith reached for her sister's hand. "Come, let us go for our people," she said. And then they got in the van, which "drove off, no one knew where."

SIXTEEN

JOURNEY'S END

Within a week, Edith and Rosa were dead, suffocated in the gas chamber at Auschwitz. There were few witnesses to the final week of their journey and none to their murder. In fact, it wasn't until 1950 that the *Dutch Gazette*, in publishing the names of all those deported at the same time as Edith and Rosa, noted their deaths on August 9 at Auschwitz. Eight years later, the Red Cross in the Netherlands provided official confirmation of this sad fact. Given the overwhelming number of Jews killed by the Nazis and the sheer volume of wartime records, it took a long time to match conclusively the Stein sisters to a place and time of execution.

But the evidence had pointed that way from the start. On August 3, after a long journey through the night (the driver had taken a wrong turn), Edith and Rosa arrived at Amersfort concentration camp. The guards gave them a rough welcome, beating them on the back with truncheons as they entered a hut to sleep. They were at Amersfort less than a day, but found other religious interred there and joined them to pray the Divine Office and the rosary. In the middle of the night, the authorities shipped Edith and Rosa and over a thousand other Jews and Catholic Jews to the transit camp of Westerbork.

The prisoners were at Westerbork for only three days, but witnesses remembered Edith's calm, comforting presence. A Dutch man who worked there later recalled that from the moment he met Edith, he knew that "here is someone truly great."

> For a couple of days she lived in that hellhole, walking, talking and praying ... like a saint. And she really was one. That is the only way to describe this middle-aged woman who struck everyone as so young, who was so whole and honest and genuine.... Talking with her was like ... journeying into another world.[1]

A Jewish prisoner who survived the war testified that Edith "was just like an angel, going around amongst the women, comforting them, helping them and calming them." Most of the mothers neglected their families and sat around "in dumb despair. [Edith] took care of the little children, washed them and combed them, looked after their feeding and their other needs.... She followed one act of charity with another until everyone wondered at her goodness."[2]

The prisoners were allowed to write brief letters, and Edith wrote several to Echt requesting supplies such as blankets, ration cards, prayer books, a toothbrush, and warm underwear. She also asked for the unfinished manuscript of *The Science of the Cross*. To one note, she attached a request for the Swiss consul to expedite the necessary forms allowing them to emigrate to Switzerland.

Edith assured the nuns that she and Rosa were "very calm and cheerful.... Now we have a chance to experience a little how to live purely from within." "So far," Edith wrote, "I have been able to pray magnificently." Rosa enclosed a note with one of Edith's letter's saying that they had slept "very little" but were "not at all" upset.

The nuns at Echt put together a package of supplies, and two local men offered to deliver the goods. They arrived at Westerbork on

August 6, the last day the sisters spent there. The men, allowed to meet with Edith and Rosa, described their few minutes together as overwhelming.

After shaking hands, "it was some time before anyone could get any words out." Edith "quietly and calmly described everyone's troubles but her own.... Her deep faith created about her an atmosphere" of confident serenity, the men reported, and she was particularly happy that so much of the day "was free for prayer."[3]

Early on the morning of August 7, guards loaded the prisoners on a train bound for Auschwitz. Shortly after the transport entered Germany, the train stopped at the Schifferstadt station. The stationmaster, Valentine Fouquet, heard a woman call him through a crack in a sealed compartment. It was Edith.

Did he know the family of Dean Schwind? she asked. When he said he did, she asked him to pass along her greetings. Tell him, she said, that she was on her way "to the east."

She was never heard from again.

The Aftermath

For years, Edith and Rosa's friends and family cherished the hope that the two had survived. For the duration of the war and a long time after, anything approaching an organized inquiry was out of the question. Allied bombing destroyed the Cologne Carmel in 1944, "except for a room in the cellar where the sisters were on their knees expecting death at any minute."

The nuns at Echt had to flee in 1945 and ended up temporarily at a small convent in a neighboring town. They had enough presence of mind, when leaving Echt, to carry away two bags full of Edith's writings. In the confusion and bombing that followed, however, the bags were left lying in the open and then lost. Two months later, a search party of religious set out to find them and discovered the papers strewn around the ground at the convent where the nuns from Echt first stopped.

Although her writings had survived, the hard fact was that Edith had not. She had anticipated her death, but she left the Carmel at Echt with no clear idea of where the Nazis were taking her and what they had in mind. The uncertainty of even her final departure reflected the uncertainty that shadowed most of the major turning points in her life.

She went forward, as always, confident that God was with her but unable to see where she was going or to what end. "As Jesus, in his abandonment before death, delivered himself into the hands of the invisible and incomprehensible God," she wrote in *The Science of the Cross*, "the soul must do likewise—casting herself headlong into the pitch darkness of faith, the only way to the incomprehensible God."[4]

In the end, the philosopher and mystic gave herself up to the mystery that had consumed her life: The Truth that lives outside of time and beyond evil drew her, finally, from the darkness of faith into the light of eternity.

Notes

Introduction

1. S. Payne Best, *The Venlo Incident* (London: Hutchison, 1950), 186.
2. Best, 186.
3. General-Kommissar Schmidt, as quoted in Teresia de Spiritu Sancto, *Edith Stein* (New York: Sheed and Ward, 1952), 209.

One
The Road to the Future

1. Edith Stein, *Life in a Jewish Family: An Autobiography*, L. Gelber and Romaeus Leuwen, eds., Josephine Koeppel, trans. (Washington, D.C.: ICS, 1986), 59. Chapters one through eight of *Meet Edith Stein* are largely based on this autobiography and family memoir by Stein. Quotes in those chapters are also from that book unless otherwise stated.
2. Waltraud Herbstrith, *Edith Stein: A Biography*, Bernard Bonowitz, trans. (San Francisco: Ignatius, 1985), 73.

Three
A Family Like Any Other

1. Susanne Batzdorff, *Aunt Edith: The Jewish Heritage of a Catholic Saint* (Springfield, Ill.: Templegate, 1998), 71.

Four
The Seeker of Truth

1. Stein, 195–196.

Five
Philosophy, 24/7

1. Stein, 260–261.

Six
Despair and the Academic

1. Stein, 294.
2. Stein, 297.

Eight
Back on Track

1. Stein, 376–377.

Nine
The Truth at Last

1. Edith Stein, *Self-Portrait in Letters, 1916–1942.* by L. Gelber and Michael Linssen eds., Josephine Koeppel, trans. (Washington, D.C.: ICS, 1993), 5. Unless otherwise noted, the quotes from Edith's letters are drawn from this source.
2. Stein, *Self-Portrait in Letters 1916–1942,* 22.

3. Teresia de Spiritu Sancto, 59.
4. Herbstrith, 146.
5. Herbstrith, 58.
6. Josephine Koeppel, *Edith Stein: Philosopher and Mystic* (Collegeville, Minn.: Liturgical Press, 1990), 67.
7. Herbstrith, 50.
8. Teresia de Spiritu Sancto, 64.

Ten
Nearly a Nun, But Not Quite

1. Teresia de Spiritu Sancto, 66. Edith's visit to her family and years at Speyer are based on material in this book, the first biography of Stein ever published. It was written by Edith's novice mistress and, later, prioress.
2. Herbstrith, 89.
3. Teresia de Spiritu Sancto, 70.
4. Stein, *Life in a Jewish Family*, 234.
5. Teresia de Spiritu Sancto, 76.

Eleven
Living at the Hand of the Lord

1. Edith Stein, *Woman*, 2nd ed., Freda Mary Oben, trans. (Washington, D.C.: ICS, 1996), 157. All references herein to the topic of "woman" are drawn from this work, a collection of essays written by Stein and delivered as lectures between 1928 and 1932.
2. Stein, *Woman*, 165–166.
3. Stein, *Woman*, 56.
4. Teresia de Spiritu Sancto, 83.

Twelve
The Future Breaks In

1. Teresia de Spiritu Sancto, 117.
2. Teresia de Spiritu Sancto, 118.
3. Edith Stein, *The Hidden Life: Essays, Meditations, Spiritual Texts,* L. Gelber and Michael Linssen, eds., Waltraut Stein, trans. (Washington, D.C.: ICS), 92.
4. Herbstrith, 115–116.

Thirteen
Carmel: A Perfect Fit

1. Teresia de Spiritu Sancto, 127. The story of Edith's parting from her family and year in the Cologne Carmel are drawn from pages 125–185 of this book.
2. Teresia de Spiritu Sancto, 137.
3. Teresia de Spiritu Sancto, 155–156.
4. Stein, *Self-Portrait in Letters, 1916–1942,* 188.
5. Stein, *Self-Portrait in Letters, 1916–1942,* 177.
6. Stein, *Self-Portrait in Letters, 1916–1942,* 238.

Fourteen
No Longer Safe

1. Stein, *Self-Portrait in Letters, 1916–1942,* 250.
2. Stein, *Self-Portrait in Letters, 1916–1942,* 288.
3. Stein, *Self-Portrait in Letters, 1916–1942,* 275.
4. Herbstrith, 139.
5. Stein, *Self-Portrait in Letters, 1916–1942,* 298.
6. Stein, *Life in a Jewish Family,* 462.

Fifteen
The World in Flames

1. Stein, *Self-Portrait in Letters, 1916–1942*, 72.
2. Stein, *The Hidden Life*, 94.
3. Stein, *The Hidden Life*, 102.
4. Stein, *The Hidden Life*, 110.
5. Stein, *Self-Portrait in Letters, 1916–1942*, 341.
6. Teresia de Spiritu Sancto, 198.
7. Herbstrith, 168.
8. Stein, *Self-Portrait in Letters, 1916–1942*, 291.
9. Teresia de Spiritu Sancto, 204–205.
10. For a description of Edith's arrest, see Teresia de Spiritu Sancto, 206–210.

Sixteen
Journey's End

1. Herbstrith, 186.
2. Teresia de Spiritu Sancto, 217.
3. Teresia de Spiritu Sancto, 213–214.
4. Edith Stein, *The Science of the Cross: A Study of St. John of the Cross,* www.ocd.pcn.net.

BIBLIOGRAPHY

Batzdorff, Susanne M. *Aunt Edith: The Jewish Heritage of a Catholic Saint.* Springfield, Ill.: Templegate, 1998.

Best, S. Payne. *The Venlo Incident.* London: Hutchison, 1950.

Graef, Hilda C. *The Scholar and the Cross.* London: Longmans, Green, 1955.

Herbstrith, Waltraud. *Edith Stein: A Biography.* Bernard Bonowitz, trans. San Francisco: Ignatius, 1985. Quoted with permission.

Koeppel, Josephine. *Edith Stein: Philosopher and Mystic.* Collegeville, Minn.: Liturgical Press, 1990.

Oben, Freda Mary. *The Life and Thought of Edith Stein.* New York: Alba House, 2001.

Stein, Edith. *The Hidden Life: Essays, Meditations, Spiritual Texts.* L. Gelber and Michael Linssen, eds.; Waltraut Stein, trans. Washington, D.C.: ICS, 1992.

_____. *Life in a Jewish Family: An Autobiography.* L. Gelber and Romaeus Leuven, eds. Josephine Koeppel, trans. Washington, D.C: ICS, 1986.

_____. *On the Problem of Empathy.* Waltraut Stein, trans. Washington, D.C.: ICS, 1989.

_____. *Self-Portrait in Letters, 1916–1942.* L. Gelber and Michael Linssen, eds. Josephine Koeppel, trans. Washington, D.C.: ICS, 1993.

_____. *The Science of the Cross: A Study of St. John of the Cross.* L. Gelber and Romaeus Leuven, eds.; Hilda Graef, trans. Chicago: Henry Regnery, 1960.

_____. *Woman.* Freda Mary Oben, trans. Washington, D.C.: ICS, 1996.

Sullivan, John, ed. *Holiness Befits Your House: Canonization of Edith Stein, A Documentation.* Washington, D.C.: ICS, 2000.

Teresia de Spiritu Sancto. *Edith Stein.* New York: Sheed and Ward, 1952.